Making Every Pitch Count

An Innovative Approach
to Retiring Hitters

**Written by Former
Pittsburgh Pirates Scouting Supervisor
Ken Beardslee**

First published by AuthorHouse 04/12/04

ISBN: 1-4140-6465-9 (e-book)
ISBN: 1-4184-3180-X (Paperback)

Library of Congress Control Number: 2004091662

This book is printed on acid free paper.

Printed in the United States of America
Bloomington, IN

Other Books by this author:

Little Field On the Corner

Kid From Connersburg

Partners

Home is Where You Hang Your Spikes

Rhymes For All Times

Life's Precious Moments in Verse

WESTERN MICHIGAN UNIVERSITY

I have known Ken for more than 20 years; first as a scout for the Pittsburgh Pirates and then as an instructor in his youth baseball camps.

I have always been impressed with Ken's knowledge of the game of baseball and particularly his knowledge and passion for pitching. He is a fine teacher and I believe that any young pitcher will benefit from this book.

Sincerely,

Fred Decker
Head Baseball Coach
Western Michigan University

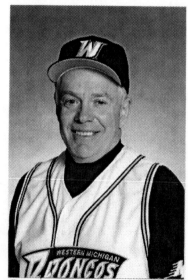

INTRODUCTION

Some years ago, I was scouting ball players down south when I was told a baseball story about a young man completely down on his luck during the post World War I days. I have looked into the story from time to time and, in my judgment, it is a true tale. It has been told and retold through the years, a little added here, a little taken away there, so I will try to reconstruct it here, with a change of names, with a challenge to my personal memory. It carried a message well worth remembering.

On a bleak rainy April afternoon, a rather tall young man in a cheap suit, wrinkled and spotted with stains, a frayed shirt, and a felt hat existing well beyond its intended life span, walked into a city bank in New York and asked to see the bank officer in charge of personal loans. After some deliberation, the man was ushered into a small office and took a seat before the bank's loan representative.

After sizing up his customer, the banker asked, "You wished to talk to me?"

The young man, with much weariness, holding his hat in his hand, began talking in a soft manner. "I've had a rough spell of it for some time, just can't find steady work. Recently I received a phone call from a dear friend, a lady friend, informing me that she would be arriving in the city to spend a single day, and wished to spend a few hours with me. I'm to meet her at a certain restaurant, share lunch with her, and then return her to the train station. I thought perhaps you might be able to give me a small loan, enough so I could buy a change of clothes, nothing fancy, perhaps an ordinary suit, shirt, and maybe a pair of shoes. My hat will clean up. I was wondering if I could work the loan off by doing some janitorial duties around the bank."

The bank officer, showing little concern, answered, "I'm afraid not. I have no authority to grant a loan under those circumstances." In a few seconds, he had vacated the office.

Out on the street, the young man walked a number of blocks until he found a park and lowered himself down on a bench, and there he sat with his hat in his hands. Nearly an hour passed, and then he felt something tapping him on the shoulder. Looking up, he saw a black cane being held by a well dressed elderly man, his rather florid face was lighted with an infectious smile.

"What seems to be the problem?" the man asked.

After a slight pause, the young man answered, "The problem I have is without a solution. I can't seem to make, or get a break."

The visitor took a seat on the bench. "Tell me the entire story", he said.

After relating the same story he had told the bank officer, he heard the older man ask, "And what is your profession?"

The young man answered, "I was a professional baseball player, a left-handed pitcher. I hurt my arm and was forced to give up baseball. I've had a little business training, but such jobs here in the city are hard to come by."

"And what is your name?" the visitor asked.

"Sam Wallace", the young man said.

The visitor pondered for a few seconds. "Sam Wallace, I recall that name. You pitched in the Federal League, compiled quite a record for a couple of seasons. You were taken from the American League about the same time Eddie Plank transferred. It had to be around 1915."

The ragged and saddened man lifted his head. "How would you know such things?"

There was no answer to the question; instead the man said kindly, "Come, join me in a ride to the country."

The odd couple arrived at their destination, a lavish estate stretching it seemed for a mile or more. The discouraged young man of the street was given a room, and in time, was supplied with a comfortable change of clothes, including a fine suit, a white shirt, new shoes, and a brand new derby. In the evening, the host and his guest sat down for a long conversation. During this visit, the left-hander learned a great deal about his benefactor. His name was George

Stovall, the owner of an east coast railroad, and the president of a baseball club in the National League.

Turning to railroad talk, the host asked, "Is your lady friend traveling by railway coach or Pullman?"

"I really don't know," the former pitcher answered.

"Well, in the coaches, I am sad to say, fine coal cinders can sometimes percolate into the seats, and lubricating oil dripping onto hot brake shoes doesn't smell the best, but the Pullmans are not like that. If your dear friend comes in on a coach, I'll see to it that she leaves in a Pullman."

Three days after that meeting in the city park, Sam Wallace met his beautiful lady friend at a well-known restaurant, and they spent an afternoon together that they both termed most delightful, and never to be forgotten.

As a final chapter, Sam Wallace was hired by George Stovall, to assist in the field and office operations of his ball club.

Getting in, and staying in, professional baseball is not an easy task. When I was injured as a player, I returned home from Lenox Hill Hospital in New York City. I worked in a bank for two years with one of my sisters. I dreamed about getting back into baseball but I knew my chances were not the best. Then one afternoon, I received a phone call from the scout who had signed me for the Yankees. He needed someone to look at free agent pitchers in Michigan. Ray Meyers had switched clubs and was now scouting for the Detroit Tigers. For one year, I helped this nice man, then I received a call from the Pittsburgh Pirates and for the next twenty years I served as a scout, eventually becoming a scouting supervisor, handling all the scouting duties in a five state area. I scouted high school and college players in Michigan, Ohio, Indiana, Kentucky, and Tennessee. In 1971, when the Pirates defeated the Baltimore club in the series, I received my World Series ring. A number of the players I signed reached the big leagues, and three went on to become either a general manager, or a manager in the big time (Murray Cook, Doug Melvin, and Terry Collins).

Everyone needs to have a special dream. Something far beyond personal goals, something loaded with bright stars and a glorious rainbow. There are many George Stovall's in this world, waiting to help down on their luck fellows like Sam Wallace. Many caring people have helped me along the way, including managers, fellow players, those in the scouting business, and so many others too numerous to mention here.

Sometimes dreams take time. I have known a number of professional ballplayers who have labored for eight or nine years in the minor leagues before making it up to the parent club.

In this book, I want to help all young pitchers reach their full potential. All I ask is that the readers try my methods. Most are strange to the modern day pitcher, but one should never disregard success in any profession, and on the pitching mound my record speaks for itself.

Chapter 1

In my personal library, I have a great collection of books on the life and accomplishments of one Thomas Alva Edison, the indispensable man. There is no area of modern life that is not shaped by the creativity of this great inventor. I have often thought what if Thomas Edison had been born with a great love for baseball, along with some outstanding pitching qualities. His message for all time, as I interpret it, was that whenever possible, we must always work as a team but we must never lose our sense of uniqueness, our duty to inventiveness, never following a set pattern, always looking for new ways and new ideas to make the product more workable and less problematical. There is little doubt in my mind that, born with pitching skills, Mr. Edison would have dazzled the baseball world with countless new ways to retire the best hitters in any era.

During my many trips through the New York Yankee farm system, I can still remember every game, every rewarding experience, each disappointment, and of course, all the love I had for the game each time I toed the rubber against the opposition. I was constantly searching for new ways to give me an edge over the best minor league hitters, and believe me, back in the 50's those leagues were loaded with outstanding batsmen. As an example of my inventiveness, I recall a game I pitched against Tampa, Florida, in the Florida International League back in the early 1950's. I limited the Tampa Club to one single and as I headed to the clubhouse after the contest, the center fielder for Tampa stopped me and said, "You really had that slider working tonight, Ken. I congratulate you, it was unhitable." He was a true gentleman, a sportsman to be remembered, and to be mentioned here. The irony of this story is that I have never thrown a slider in my life during an official game. The reason being I always had an outstanding curveball. Years after my game in Tampa, Mayo Smith told me during one of our scouting trips (Mayo managed for years in the Yankee system and then years later managed the Detroit Tigers to a world championship) that I had the best late breaking curveball he had ever seen. A few years earlier I had struck out eighteen Dodger farmhands in a game at Independence, Kansas, in the K.O.M. league.

Getting back to the Tampa game, what I was throwing instead of a slider was an off center fastball that would slide off the outside corner to a right-handed hitter. I also used it to get in on the hands of a left-handed hitter. Today it is called a "cut fastball" but back in the 50's very few pitchers had it in their arsenal. I would never badmouth the slider as a respectable pitch, but in my judgment, it is a poor substitute for a late breaking, good rotation curveball. The secret to the effectiveness of any breaking pitch is the bite (quick and tight rotation) and the location. With good sound mechanics, and determination, the talented pitcher will seldom ever hang his curveball. I always kept the pitch at the knees, or a bit below. Many hitters will chase the pitch out of the strike zone. The slider is a fine pitch if it can be kept down and out of the sweet hitting zone. Unfortunately, it often is up and has too much of the plate. I can't prove the statement, but I would say more long balls are hit off the slider than any other pitch. Many pitchers have problems throwing a decent curveball (thick wrists and heavy forearms). As you might guess, they turn to the slider, which is not an easy pitch on the arm.

An old timer once told me that the first thing for a young pitcher to decide is the grips to be used on the baseball. I totally agree. Don't ask me why, but it is true that most pitchers' arms react in different ways to the various grips on the baseball. A young pitcher of sixteen years of age should find a catcher, perhaps a buddy down the street, warm up slowly, and then start experimenting. Throw half a dozen fastballs across the wide seams, another half dozen across the narrow seams, then with the seams, then with a grip a little off center. Use a slight change of finger pressure and see what happens. Both you and your catcher watch the movement. As we all know, a straight fastball, whatever the velocity, is easy to hit for the accomplished hitter. Show me a smart pitcher, an 88 mile per hour fastball with movement and location, a change off his fastball, and a couple of changes on his curveball, and I'll show you a winner in any league.

Never throw any pitch that does not have movement. In my days in the Yankee system, I saw many pitchers with a high velocity fastball. The Yankee farmhands, right-handers and left-handers, were noted for their ability to really pop a catcher's mitt. However, most never made AAA or the parent club for the good breaking ball was absent, the fastball was too straight, or good control was a problem. In still a later chapter, I will discuss the great importance of throwing strikes. When I was scouting, an area of five states, I would see part of maybe 500-600 games and a countless amount of young pitchers. I saw all the problems, and control was a factor with most of these young hopefuls. You cannot win at any level unless you stay ahead of the hitters in the count.

In this book, I will refer often to my own record as an amateur and professional pitcher. The numbers I bring forth are accurate, straight from the box scores in my office. I use them for reference for I know if young pitchers will listen they will greatly improve their natural talents. Many of the theories I developed and put to use to win, you will not find elsewhere, not in books, or in the spoken word.

Following is my pitching record for a period of nine seasons. At the age of 24, I suffered a career ending back injury, and thereafter was unable to pitch a single inning.

High school – 3 seasons, 25 wins and a single loss.
8 no-hitters, including 2 perfect games (national record).
26 strikcouts in a 10 inning game; 25 strikeouts in a 9 inning game (Michigan state record).
20 strikeouts in a seven inning game (Michigan state record).
18 strikeouts for every 21 batters faced (career) (national record).
19 strikeouts for every 21 batters faced senior year (national record).
Other amateur games, 27 wins and 6 losses.

Professional record in the New York Yankee system – 64 wins and 24 losses. Included in the wins were 7 one hitters, and two games in which I struck out 18 hitters in a nine inning game.

3

Two years in the United States Army in which I pitched for the Camp Rucker, Alabama ball club, one of the finest service teams in the nation (Spud Chandler, a former great Yankee pitcher was scouting that particular area for the Yankees and attended many of the games in which I pitched. Later he was to invite me to the Yankee rookie camp in Lake Wales, Florida where the best 25 Yankee farmhands were able to show their stuff). At Camp Rucker, we won the Alabama-Georgia-Florida championship, and then traveled to Wichita, Kansas to play in the National NBC championship tourney.

Record at Rucker 40 wins and two losses.
Total record for 9 seasons – 156 wins and 33 losses.

Did I have an arm that threw the baseball with greater velocity than most professional pitchers? I do not believe so. There were no timing devices for velocity in those days but I probably topped out at around 92 miles per hour. I did have an outstanding breaking ball, and pinpoint control, but others could make the same statement. The others, however, seldom ever reached my winning percentage. At Norfolk, Virginia in the Piedmont League, I went 17-4. Whitey Ford, a couple of years earlier, went 16-8. So what made the difference?

Anyone who is close to me knows that I seldom ever talk about what I accomplished in baseball. It has always made me uncomfortable; however with this publication, I have the opportunity to help young pitchers. Baseball, and pitching in particular, can be a very cruel endeavor. I have seen many pitchers booed off the mound by a very impatient audience. I have been witness to grown men crying in the clubhouse after a rough outing. With the proper training, the correct information, and sound theories, a young pitcher can bypass all these trying times and advance to the top of any league he so wishes.

I always felt, when on the mound, that I was better than the hitter in the batter's box. You must have that degree of confidence to win in great competition. When I had my good stuff, I felt I could beat any club, anywhere. In the mid 1950's, I faced the New York Yankees in an exhibition game at Birmingham, Alabama. I was pitching for the AA farm club, the Birmingham Barons. The Yankees were shelling our starter and I was called into the game in the first inning with the bases loaded and but one out. As I took my warm up pitches, I noticed the great former St. Louis Cardinal star, Enos Country Slaughter, taking his practice swings in the on-deck circle. Slaughter had spent 15 years with the Cardinals before moving on to the Yankees. He left that club with a 300 lifetime batting average. I had read all about his baseball feats as a lad growing up in Michigan, and all baseball fans knew of his dash to home plate, scoring from first on a single, to win the World Series against the Boston Red Sox. Now I was facing him with the bases packed.

I took a step off the mound, gathered my thoughts, making sure I was charting a sound course, and then took my sign. I was determined to give Enos something to think about. I knew with the bases loaded and my wanting to get ahead in the count that he would be looking for a fastball. Instead, I got a curveball sign from my catcher, Mo Thacker (who would later catch for the Chicago Cubs), and this pitch seemed to confuse the Yankee outfielder. He took a weak swing at the pitch low and inside and hit a nice four or five hopper to our second baseman, Jerry Lumpe (who later played for the Yankees, the Kansas City A's, and the Detroit Tigers). Jerry and our shortstop turned the double play and the inning was over.

Again, what an advantage it is for any pitcher to be able to throw a breaking ball for a strike at any point in the count. No set patterns.

Although I will discuss the first inning and its importance later in another chapter, I do want to touch on it here for a brief period. I have always thought that the first inning was the most important of all the innings. The pitcher must be prepared to face the difficult part of the batting order. The lead-off man; a good solid two spot hitter; and then the meat of the order containing the power; the third and then followed by the clean-up hitter. A couple of slip-ups and your club has to play catch up. I have the feeling that more runs are scored in the first inning than any other in the game. Lack of preparedness; jitters; poor pitch selection; all contribute to first inning disasters. I may be off a game or so over my professional game experiences but I would say I can count on one hand the times I gave up a run in the opening inning.

Again, be inventive, dare to be different, be deceptive, no set patterns. In the 1946 All Star Game, Ted Williams, the Boston Red Sox slugger, faced a National League pitcher by the name of Rip Sewell. Sewell was a fine pitcher for the Pittsburgh Pirates, and ended his career with a respectable 143-97 record. Rip had great imagination on the mound and had invented what he called the "epheus" pitch. It was a slow pitch with the apex of its arch toward the plate some thirty feet in the atmosphere. The general feeling was that a farmer could drive a load of hay under it. Sewell threw the pitch to Williams and for the first time ever it was deposited in the right field stands for a homerun. Rip frequently got the pitch over for a strike, but rarely was anybody foolish enough to swing at it.

Well, my young baseball friends, this seems quite enough to digest for one chapter. Let's take a pause, do some serious thinking, perhaps take a few notes, and then move on to chapter 2.

Grips
1st pitch
1st inning

Chapter 2

A number of years ago, while a scouting supervisor for the Pittsburgh Pirates, I came across a slender left-handed high school pitcher in the Detroit area. I kept returning to see him for I knew he was something very special. In those days, the front office would at times send a special assignment scout to double check certain prospects. The Pirates had a wonderful gentleman by the name of George Detour and I picked him up at the Detroit airport and drove him out to the field where the kid was scheduled to pitch. I had talked with other scouts and no one seemed very interested in the southpaw's abilities. With my background as a successful pitcher, I always felt I had an advantage over other scouts who had been non pitchers. To shorten a long story, George watched the lefty pitch one inning and then said, "I've seen enough." Back in the car I thought for sure I had brought this veteran scout to see someone he totally disliked as a prospect. Down the road a piece, I asked his opinion. He remarked, "I like him. Smart, sets his entire game up around his curveball. Probably throws 87 at best but his fastball sinks and after his slow stuff, it looks like a 90 miler."

The little lefty was signed and reported to the Western Carolina League, which he set right on its ear. If memory serves me correctly, he went 13-2 or something like that. In a season and a half, he was in AAA. I wish I could say he had the opportunity to face big league hitters, but like so many others coming through the minor leagues, he was injured and left active playing. I still believe he might have been the best prospect I ever signed, and I signed a number that have made me very proud.

Every young pitcher must accurately evaluate his talent. He must decide what happens to be his best pitch, use it for a foundation, a starting point, and then build his entire product around it. In my case, I felt my curveball was a stronger weapon than my fastball. Wherever I pitched, I used my curveball for my strikeout pitch, and so many times I merely showed the hitter the fastball to set him up for the over-hand bender.

I have many parents and young pitchers ask me if it is a must to throw 90 miles per hour to be considered a pro prospect, or even a college prospect. First let me say it is a great advantage to have a 90 mile per hour fastball. The velocity sets up all of your other pitches, especially your change of speed deliveries. Scouts for professional baseball love velocity. At times they are fooled badly by young pitchers like the lefty I mentioned earlier. They fail to look at the entire picture, especially the boy's baseball aptitude. The first time I actually saw Whitey Ford pitch (in an exhibition game against our club in the Piedmont League), I was not impressed with his velocity, probably 88 that day, and that might be stretching it a little. But I watched him closely and I soon understood why he won so often as he had a great curveball that he could throw for a strike at anytime, pinpoint control, and he was a master at taking a little off or putting a little extra on his fastball and curveball. He had worked hard on his fielding, his motion to first base, his bunting, and his hitting. His pitches seldom caught too much of the plate. I realized he got the absolute most out of his God given baseball talent.

May I ask how hard do you wish to work to become a great pitcher? So many young pitchers have good arms but to what degree are they building upon their natural talents. So many I used to scout stood at about 50%, some even lower. When I was in high school, I watched all the good pitchers that came to town to play on Sunday afternoons. The town where I was raised was small but the local players, may of them farmers, knew how to play this American game. Strong teams would visit from Battle Creek, Lansing, Jackson, and Grand Rapids. When I was fifteen years of age, I was asked to join the team, and the following year became a regular member of the pitching staff. I would carefully study the opposing men on the mound. Some were ex-minor league players. I picked up all kinds of useful information studying their wind-ups; their stretch positions; their pitch selection; and so many other fine pitching points. I would write all of this down in a small notebook at the close of the day.

From watching and then pitching in those games, I knew control and throwing strikes, could surely make the difference between success and failure. I decided to improve my control by building a contraption that, by today's standards, would be outright crude. But it worked – and how it worked! I would strongly recommend it today. To start with, I put two wooden stakes in the ground about seven feet apart, straight across from each other. I then got some lightweight white string and put a line from stake to stake right at the level I judged to be the lower part of the strike zone (knees for an average height hitter). Then I did the same arrangement at the top of the strike zone. Closing out, I ran two vertical pieces of string the width of home plate. Tying the strings together, I now had an enclosed area of the strike zone. Throwing to a catcher behind the stringed box, I could now work on not only throwing within the box but actually trying to hit the string representing the corners of the plate and the horizontal levels at the top and lower sections of the strike zone. I practiced for hours whenever I could find a catcher, and later on in pro baseball it seemed I could still see that string helping me into the strike zone. During my years in high classification baseball, I pitched a number of games without a base on balls. I can well remember one game in Havana, Cuba, against a Washington Senator farm club, when I pitched 12 innings without a walk.

In this chapter, I want to mention a few other unusual tricks that did wonders for me. I would have a buddy who was not playing a particular day do me a good turn. I would ask him to watch the opposing hitters while I pitched and put a mark on a piece of paper every time one of them took a level swing, that is when they failed to lift their hands to swing at a pitch above the waist, or when they likewise failed to lower their hands to swing at a low pitch. The reason being that anytime a hitter is able to take a level swing you are dealing in his wheelhouse. If the pitch has too much of the plate you're in real trouble. Anytime you make the hitter raise or lower his hands I believe you have a much better chance of getting him out. I noticed that when fewer marks were on my buddy's piece of paper, I had pitched a better game. It takes some added effort from a buddy but it pays off during the course of an entire season.

Something else that really helped my performance was my pre-game warm up. While taking my fifteen minutes to get ready for the game, I would actually pitch a couple of innings in the bullpen.

After I was loose I would visualize the lead-off hitter stepping into the box. Then I would mix my pitches up as if the game had started. Same for the second, third, and clean-up hitter. When the actual game started, I felt I was more than ready to mix my pitches up, and to throw strikes. I have watched many pro pitchers warm up by throwing four fastballs in a row; three curveballs or sliders; and two or three change pitches, something they probably would never do in a regular game. Remember what I said earlier about the amount of runs scored in the first inning.

Moving on to another helper. When you're facing good hitters at any level, study each hitter as they step into the box. Perhaps during an earlier game when you were on the bench you had the opportunity to take note of where each hitter stood in the box. Does he have complete bat coverage of the strike zone? Does he have a hitch in his swing, or for some other reason does he take too long to get his hands started, the bat moving in contact with the ball? Does he have a blind spot inside the strike zone? Does he over swing, or pull off the plate? Does he crowd the plate? Will he chase certain pitches out of the strike zone?

In 1954, I was pitching a game in Havana, Cuba (Washington Senator farm club, Class B International League). Their right fielder was a player by the name of Julio Becquer, a left-handed hitter. I noticed the game before I pitched that he had a small blind spot in the strike zone. When I faced him the next night, I pinpointed a number of pitches in that area and he went hitless. All toll, I faced him ten times and he never recorded a base hit. The Senators brought him up the following year and he stayed around for six or seven seasons. His big league hitting average was 244, so I always felt someone else spotted the same weakness that I discovered.

Another helper. The straight change is making a comeback in the big leagues and in college baseball. It was always there for me. It is a must for any successful pitcher. Young pitchers often scoff at the idea of changing speeds. It is a very difficult pitch to master for it takes a great deal of patience and hard work. Some pitchers get hurt with the pitch in a game and refuse to stick with it. I loved the straight change and I always used it against the heavy hitters, swing hitters that took a little more stride, hitters with a little more loop in their swing. I used it effectively against Jim Gentile in the Southern Association, and Jim Lemon of the same league. Later Gentile hit 46

10

homeruns for the 1961 Baltimore Orioles. Jim Lemon hit 27 homeruns for the Senators in 1956. Gentile was a great fastball hitter, but he could be fooled with good motion off-speed pitches. Lemon, who played for Chattanooga, had great power when I was with Birmingham. I never challenged him with a fastball in the strike zone. I had good luck getting him out with curveballs and now and then a changeup after a show me fastball. By all means, add this pitch to your arsenal. It's easy on the arm and very hard on the hitter.

Pitching inside. I found out early in my pitching career that I had to pitch inside to make my best pitch, the curveball, effective. Hitters, the right-handed ones, started leaning across the plate to take a good swipe at my strikeout pitch. They were taking the outside corner away from me. But not for long. When I caught such a hitter cheating, I came inside with a good 92 mile per hour heater. Not to hit him but to move him off the plate. I kept the pitch away from his head, although I can well remember hitting a hitter or two on the arm. The word soon gets around the league that you will come inside and then most of the leaning across the plate will stop. I've noticed a number of pitchers who are still reluctant to move a hitter off the plate. With the present rules in the big leagues for dismissal from the game if, in the umpire's judgment, you were throwing with intent to injure a hitter, I'm sure there are some pitchers who feel coming inside is not worth the risk. There is a proper time for everything that happens in our great game and what we are discussing here is a fine example. I never even thought about knocking a hitter down because he happened to hit a homerun off of me. I probably made a mistake with my location and the hitter managed an advantage. At times, you must give a good hitter credit for not only hitting a mistake, but for hitting a very good pitch. As a close observer of any game, I have noticed that when the catcher moves out from behind the plate and sets up inside (that is, he sets up a target with his body, not with the glove), on many occasions the pitch will hit the hitter. In my judgment, the catcher should always remain directly behind the plate with his setup. In past years, and all during my playing career, this was the case. He gave an inside target with the glove, but remained in his usual setup behind the plate. Anytime you change that setup, you risk a wild pitch from the mound. Only in recent years have we seen catchers moving from left to right before the delivery. It makes no sense whatsoever to me, and if I were pitching today, my catcher would stay put.

What a great student you have been. Now, put the book aside, relax a little, take a few deep breaths, perhaps have a cool drink, and then we will proceed to chapter 3.

Evaluate your best pitches
Stay off the plate
Throw inside
Evaluate hitters:
    Wheelhouse
    hand movement
    P. 10
C - behind plate -

Chapter 3

Pitchers, especially at the professional level, are an odd bunch. I've known a few who would go out and pitch their game, and when their work was over, they would take off the uniform, shower, dress, and leave the clubhouse without a word to anyone. It seems they deliberately cultivated an air of mystery. The ones that I knew were really never antisocial; I guess I would say they were self-sufficient. They felt they needed no one to lean on. Pitching was their business and while at the park they could care less what a third baseman, or an outfielder, thought about their performance, especially if they had experienced a bad outing. After all, this pitching racket is a bit unfair right from the get-go.

Pitchers stand in the middle of the diamond with a target on their chest. Hitters despise them and delight in lining the ball right up the middle. One must remember that a pitcher is but 55 feet from the plate after he delivers his pitch. They are totally disgraced by always being placed 9th in the batting order even though some are very good hitters. If they even twitch after a pause in their stretch position, they are called for a balk, a term more commonly used to describe a non-cooperative horse. Then, of course we have the pitching coach walking out to the mound before thousands of fans and lecturing the pitcher like a spoiled little kid. If it's not the pitching coach, it's the manager, who of course, never takes an infielder to task for a foul up, only the poor pitcher. Then when the pitcher gets into a little jam late in the game, here the manager comes again, takes the ball, and says something like, "Don't use too much of the hot water." Is it any wonder I decided to write a book to help these poor fellows.

So, dear readers, let's take some space and discuss how a young pitcher can help himself by becoming an accomplished fielder;

a respectable hitter; a sound bunter; and have the ability to keep runners close. If I do not have enough room in this chapter to cover all of these items, I will let them overflow into chapter 4.

First, let's discuss fielding. It seems every time I watch a game on TV or attend a game in a minor or big league park, I witness a pitcher throwing a ball away either on a slow topper, or a bunt. The number one mistake is throwing the ball while off-balanced, falling across the first baseline and either hitting the runner in the back, or heaving the ball down into the right field corner. Another problem is lobbing the ball to the first baseman instead of putting something on the throw. Many pitchers take fielding for granted. Why it's easy – after all, it's a slow rolling ball with a short throw to first base. Oh yes, they practice covering first base on a ground ball to the first baseman, but fail to practice fielding slow hoppers and bunts. I played nearly four years in the minor leagues and never made a single error. Unbelievable you say? Not at all, when you consider that many other pitchers performed just as well because they practiced those plays.

Starting a double play by throwing to second base after a ground ball near the mound is another play that takes practice. It's all proper timing based on how quickly the batted ball reaches the pitcher. Get in touch with your shortstop and second baseman and let them know they can count on a chest high throw at the bag. You can help yourself with a double play, or, end up with base runners on first and third. Good fielding pitchers are yet another spoke in the wheel of a well-greased infield.

Hitting. Isn't it pathetic to watch big league, minor league, or college pitchers at the plate? Is it wrong to expect a pitcher to at least get his bat on the ball, hitting a ground ball or a fly ball? How can so many productive pitchers on the mound be so helpless when they have a bat in their hands?

I'm not going to compare myself, hitting wise, to the average amateur or professional pitcher as I could have been signed as an infielder, but the fact remains that any pitcher able to make a little contact can certainly win some games for himself. If a pitcher makes an honest effort at the plate, gets a base hit now and then, and has the ability to move base runners along with a sacrifice, the manager will think twice about replacing him with another pitcher.

Almost all pitchers, when facing the opposing pitcher with a bat in his hand, will start him off with a fastball. The reason being he has better control with the fastball than a breaking pitch. So, as a hitter you guess fastball, making sure the pitch is a strike, and make contact. If you miss the first pitch, be patient. The odds are you will see a couple more fastballs while you're in the box. In my case, I always took the curveballs unless I had two strikes against me. No pitcher I ever knew was a good breaking ball hitter. You do not have enough trips to the plate to solve hitting that difficult pitch. I always guessed fastball and during my minor league career, hit a number of homeruns off non thinking pitchers. In a game against Nashville, in the AA Southern Association, I actually hit a grand slam on a first pitch fastball. Here are a few other very important pointers on hitting. Make sure you have complete bat coverage of the plate. Develop a compact swing with no big loops. Do not over-swing. I never went up to the plate swinging for a homerun. If a pitcher has a good live fastball and you take a nice level, compact swing, the ball can leave the ballpark. The pitcher supplies the power. When I was facing a decent hitting pitcher, I would tempt him now and then with a fastball at the letters. As a hitting pitcher you must lay off that high heater. Even good position hitters have trouble catching up with that pitch. Another suggestion I would like to mention here is that if you have two strikes against you, cut down on your swing even more than I mentioned earlier. You might prevent another strikeout.

Bunting. To be truthful, it seems to be a lost art even for the position players. The pitcher, of course, is not bunting for a base hit but rather sacrificing a runner or runners along. To begin with, get a good pitch to bunt; nothing above the waist, for those pitches more than likely will be bunted into the air. Square around, bend at the knees, get a waist high, or a knee high pitch to bunt, and let the bat do the work. Never jab at the pitch, let the pitch come to the bat and give with your hands to deaden the ball. Never drop the head of the bat. Another point for remembrance, do not try to be too fine by bunting the ball close to the foul line. Three or maybe four feet will be adequate. If you try to be too fine, the ball will probably roll into foul territory. Once you lay the ball down, get to first base as quickly as possible. If the bunt is a little too hard, there could be a quick throw to second base and back to first for a double play.

When we had a day off in professional baseball, a number of hardworking pitchers would visit the ball park and practice their bunting. I can well remember one drill I always worked on at these

15

sessions. With a base runner at second base, or with runners at second and first, the bunter should make the third baseman field the ball. All of these tips are basic points. What I want to impress on the reader is the need for practice to improve the pitcher's performance. Again, get a buddy to throw you some high and low pitches, and as I mentioned earlier, lay off the high ones and work on bunting the low ones. If you can find a buddy to help who can throw in the mid-eighties or so, that of course is ideal. You might have to buy your buddy lunch, as I have done time after time, but the rewards are endless.

Keeping base runners close. Even in the big leagues we can see the shortcomings of pitcher after pitcher in this phase of pitching. I always had three good moves to first base and at one time or the other all were effective. Let's run through some dos and don'ts of keeping base runners honest.

Let's look at the do list first. Do pay attention to the base runner unless he happens to be a very slow runner, or a pitcher. In that instance, give just about all of your attention to the hitter. Why waste a throw to first base that might be in the dirt allowing such a runner to advance a base. Do throw over when you have a base runner that is capable of getting a running lead, or a walking lead, during any part of the game. Never give him your best move on the first throw, that comes later. Do vary your moves in speed and method. Again, we're talking about the danger of patterns. If he reads you well, your catcher has little chance of throwing him out. If you're a right-hander, eliminate the high leg kick with your left leg. I do not like the slide step, barely moving the front foot off the ground. With no leg kick whatsoever, a great deal of velocity can be lost in the delivery. Instead, compromise and split the difference. Do keep the throws to your first baseman knee high so he has the opportunity for a quick tag. What a wasted effort it is to throw chest high in such instances. Do know all the balk rules regarding your moves to first base. Read them over and over again.

With a base runner at second, always have a pickoff play with your shortstop and second baseman. Never throw the ball if there's no chance of retiring the runner. Again, watch his lead, and then, as we discussed when a base runner is on first, compromise on the leg kick and make your delivery to the plate. You cannot balk at second base by not completing your throw, that also pertains to third base. Always remember that the pitcher's main focus should be on the hitter.

Pitchers who worry too much about base runners are soon out of the game, out of the league. Left-handers should always be able to keep runners close at first base. No excuses. You're looking right in his eyes and there's no reason he should ever get a walking or running lead. The move with the step towards first while on the rubber is to be perfected, and also the move when you step off with your back foot and throw a quick delivery to first with little body help but a great deal of arm strength. As with right-handers, left-handers compromise on your leg kick to first base.

In my own case, I had no secrets for keeping runners close. I simply worked hard at the task, always giving my catcher a good opportunity to throw out runners. As I mentioned, do not waste throws to bases. In a later chapter, I will go into detail about wasted pitches and throws by the pitcher.

In another later chapter, I will talk of hard work and dedication in perfecting a pitcher's natural skills. I can well remember reading a story years ago regarding the great second baseman, Rogers Hornsby, and his total disdain for lack of effort and dedication. A rookie arrived in spring training while Hornsby was manager of the St. Louis Browns. This particular second baseman arrived a day late, took a dozen ground balls in the infield and then walked to the dugout. Rogers was so upset he could only sputter, "Look at him! Reports late, fields a few ground balls, and now he's all set for the season. If that were me being called up from the bushes, I'd have been here three days early, and when I went out to field my position, I would have stayed out there taking ground balls until they pulled me off the field."

Is it any wonder that Hornsby has a lifetime batting average of 358, second highest of all time, played 23 years in the big leagues, and was elected to the Hall of Fame in 1942.

Thomas Edison always said that his successes were a percentage of inspiration and perspiration. Both are equally important. Without hard work and dedication, anything I mention in this book is totally useless. When I was scouting and holding tryout camps, I noticed that some boys rode buses for hours to get to the camps. Some hitched rides, or rode bikes for miles, and some had saved their hard earned money to buy a special glove or bat, so they might make a better impression. They stayed the entire two days and gave everything they had every minute of each day. On the other hand, I saw boys with some ability that left after an hour or so, not willing to stay long enough for me to get any kind of an assessment of their talent. Needless to say, I was extremely disappointed in their attitude.

Now, let's take another little break, maybe remove your shoes, lean back and relax, and then we shall move on to chapter 4.

Chapter 4

Baseball has a long history of players having idiosyncrasies, some delightful, and others downright off the planet. It seems baseball is a profession where the abnormal is often the normal. Some pitchers make sure they never step on a baseline while coming and going from the mound. Others never want anyone to mention a no-hitter to them while the game is progressing. I knew one successful pitcher who never washed his sweatshirt for a month and a half because he won eight starts in a row in the odorant thing. For me, superstitions never had much to do with winning or losing. I was more aware of what great preparation could mean during a season.

I am a firm believer that pitchers in my era were in better shape physically than they are today. I know we did twice the running that modern pitchers do at all levels of competition. We never lifted weights, or worked out on machines. During the off season, I always ran, inside and outside, and in spring training I logged more miles than an ice cream truck in August, in Palm Springs. Running is the best way to build up leg strength, and leg strength is nearly as important as arm strength. A starting pitcher, in my mind, should be able to pitch 9 innings every 5 days without the slightest problem of fatigue. However, if his legs are not strong, about the 7th inning he starts losing his control, starts laboring, and as a result he starts hanging his curveball, or slider, and his fastball begins to tail high and away to left-handed hitters, and high and in to the right-handed hitters (I'm talking about a right-handed pitcher here). Tom Seaver, the Hall of Fame pitcher, had great stuff; he also had a pair of tremendously strong legs. He used them to push off the rubber, and to drive the rest of his body toward the hitter. Tom pitched over 4,500 innings in his career, and averaged close to 250 innings per season. He could not have accomplished such numbers without those great legs.

So, young pitchers, between starts run, run, run. The day after you pitch, you should never pick up a baseball, just pick up your feet and do some sprints. Walk a while, and then sprint some more. In my own case, I never grew tired or unsteady on my legs, as the late innings approached. In several seasons, I have had over 20 complete games per year and four times in the minor leagues I went past the 12th inning. In a later chapter, I want to discuss fully the reason the complete game has become an oddity, and why it is so important in the entire role of the successful pitcher.

In this chapter, I want to stress the importance of always accepting a challenge as you advance up the ladder in becoming a winning pitcher.

Years ago, when I was 16 years of age, I pitched during the summer months in the Lansing and Battle Creek, Michigan city leagues. There I faced older, wiser, and more talented competition. I also pitched for the town team in Vermontville, and faced strong competition in those games. I faced good college hitters, ex-minor leaguers, and outstanding semi-pro batters. What a learning experience!

Mickey Mantle, Ralph Terry, and so many of the other Yankee farmhands from the past, all benefited from that type of challenge. One must be tested to bring out the best in any profession. When I started pitching to very talented hitters, I discovered their bat speed was much greater than younger hitters. I can well remember pitching batting practice to the Detroit Tigers in old Briggs Stadium in 1948. The first hitter I faced was a big, strong left-handed hitter by the name of George Vico (6'4'', 200 pounds). I was told to throw my fastball at a decent velocity and was amazed when my first pitch was pulled about 40 feet foul off the right field line. Wow, I thought! How does anyone ever get a fastball by a hitter with that kind of bat speed? The answer, of course, is either having a fastball with 92-95 miles per hour, or have one with great movement, with a change of speeds. Facing big league hitters in batting practice opened my eyes, believe me.

Back home, I worked on movement, and a change of speeds. Few pitchers today (16 year olds) are aware of big league bat speed. Because they face only high school hitters, they are ill prepared when called upon at the age of 18 or 19 to face top college hitters, or professional hitters in class "A" leagues. Can you imagine an 18 or 19 year old pitcher, fresh out of high school, reporting to the Midwest League and facing a top draft pick from maybe the Big Ten Conference, or one of the other solid baseball leagues in the college ranks? Many go through that experience and many are hit so hard that they lose all their confidence. One must remember that half the professional baseball draft picks are high school players.

When I was 18 years of age, I pitched my first professional game against Lima, Ohio in the Ohio-Indiana League. I won 9-0, gave up but 5 hits, walked a single batter, and struck out 12. I was injured in the game by a careless base runner, but I finished the game. Looking back, I could not have turned in that performance without the experience of facing top amateur hitters in Lansing and Battle Creek, and in my home town of Vermontville.

So, what can I suggest to young pitchers now in high school? To begin with, make a supreme effort to be placed on a pitching staff facing better hitters than what you will see in high school. Perhaps you can find a city league team in your area that needs another arm. It will not be easy finding such a club, but it's well worth the search. If a higher classification cannot be found, you must self-educate yourself. That's where I come in with the many little gems I will mention within the pages of this book.

In high school, you will find that many hitters swing at pitches out of the strike zone. As you get into better baseball, hitters will take those pitches and you will find yourself always behind in the count. So, to begin with, you must perfect your control. Remember the homemade device I used years ago? Well, build one and put it to use. You need but two pitches in high school, your fastball and your breaking pitch, either a curveball or a slider. What happened to the straight change you ask? I never threw a change off my fastball in high school because the hitters had such slow bat speed. Yes, I worked on the pitch, and yes, I used it against older and more talented summer league hitters, but I never served it up to unskilled high school hitters. If you have a good arm, give them a good moving fastball in a good location, and a breaking pitch low in the strike zone.

When possible, watch as many successful pitchers as you can on TV. The camera angle gives the viewer an excellent opportunity to watch the movement of the pitches. Take close note of a pitcher who works the hitters in and out, up and down. No pitcher in professional baseball today will get the letter high fastball from an umpire, but that high fastball with good velocity and movement is a great two strike, no ball pitch. It's a temptation pitch and many hitters cannot lay off it. As a TV viewer, study the pitchers with a smooth fluid delivery. They can stay in a game longer for they usually have great control.

At this point, I would like to say something about the windup and its importance to a pitcher's success. Years ago, the Yankees had a big right-handed pitcher by the name of Bob Turley. They obtained him from Baltimore where, in1954, he was 14 and 15, pitching 247 innings, and walking 181 batters while striking out 185. Needless to say, this is a horrible ratio. So, when the Yankees got him, they decided to eliminate his windup and let him throw almost like an infielder off the mound. In 1958, he pitched 246 innings and walked but 128 for the Yankees, not the best, but quite an improvement. For Turley the no windup worked; it cured some of his wildness.

In explanation, when I say no windup, I mean throwing the delivery as an infielder might throw the baseball from third base to first base. In my day, most pitchers from the windup had a high leg kick, a great rotation of the hips, and a strong push off the rubber with their legs. Go back and look at some photographs of Dizzy Dean, Bob Feller, Juan Marichal, and a host of other great pitchers. The big windup was a factor in their ability to fool the best hitters in baseball. Ask any thinking hitter and he will tell you that one of the secrets in becoming a consistent hitter is seeing the ball as soon as possible from the pitcher's hand. The big windup allowed the pitcher to hide the ball a little longer, and of course, the main reason for the big windup was allowing the pitcher to use his entire body for leverage, his hips, his back, and his upper and lower legs. As far as body leverage in today's pitching market, there is little difference between their windup motion and their stretch motion. What a savings there is on the arm when you use your entire body in a big windup. Is it any wonder that Warren Spahn threw 4800 innings in his career and Bob Feller threw nearly 4000? Meanwhile Bob Turley threw but 1700 innings.

There are many other advantages to a big windup. The constant movement is great for flexibility. No pitcher wants to stiffen up during a ballgame, so with the great movement in the windup, the pitcher is kept nice and loose.

Another great advantage of the big windup is on change of speed pitches. With a big windup, the hitter focuses in on great movement during the pitchers delivery, arms and legs. The deception with a change of speed pitch is much more devastating than when a pitcher throws quite like an infielder. Remember, a pitcher should never resemble an infielder until after he delivers the baseball.

I always had a big windup during my entire career. Dizzy Dean told me never to change my delivery. My last two years in professional baseball, I won 32 games and lost but 8. I watched a number of my fellow pitchers struggle, but only a couple asked for help. If you want to improve, never be bashful about asking a successful pitcher for advice.

My pitching friends, always remember the basic forms of learning; Reading, Observing, and Listening. Learning is an endless process, it has no age limits. I seldom ever attend a ballgame without learning something about the game. As a young pitcher, I read everything I could find about the art of pitching, and of winning. As an observer, I studied successful pitchers and picked up so many wonderful pointers that helped me set records at all levels of competition. As a good listener, I tuned in to all advice voiced by present and former pitchers. I listened, but I only used what made sense to me. You know your body, your talent, better than anyone else. You know how much desire you have for the game, how hard you wish to work, and how much pride you feel when turning in a hard-earned performance. In a winning pitcher there must be a close relationship between the mind and the heart.

It is time for another break. Check your notes, rest your eyes, and then we shall move on to chapter 5.

Chapter 5

At the time of this writing, there is a new movie to be released by the title of **SEABISCUIT**, a true tale of a gallant little horse who refused to be intimidated on the track when the chips were on the table. With a heart as large as a house, he beat the best thoroughbreds in the entire country, including the great east coast horse, **WAR ADMIRAL**. Veteran trainers in the thoroughbred business totally misjudged his potential by basing their judgment on his outer looks rather than his inner strength. I can well understand such mistakes for it often happens in the scouting of professional baseball players.

When I was scouting for the Pittsburgh Pirates, I had one of the largest scouting areas in baseball, a total of five states, and half of Ontario, Canada. It's always best to see a young prospect a number of times before making a decision as to his professional abilities, but with the unpredictable spring weather in the Midwest, I was at times forced to make up my mind after one or two viewings. I had little trouble determining the potential of a boy's arm. I did not need a reading from a radar gun to know if the pitcher had good, or great, velocity. Likewise, I had no problems determining if he had a professional curveball or slider. The control factor was never a problem. My problem was deciding how much the boy loved the game, how much fire was in his belly, and what was the size of his heart. When scouting these young high school and college pitchers, I tried to see them in game conditions such as the bases loaded in the late innings with one or nobody out. I wanted to see them pull down their caps, grit their teeth, and reach back for a little extra. I never wanted to see them aim the ball, get overly excited, or lose their composure. Emotion plays a key role in such situations and the pitcher who can remain calm, think, and make good pitches will more than likely escape disaster.

Before signing a young player for the Pirates, I sat down with him and we had a lengthy conversation about how he started playing baseball, why he chose the sport over basketball, football, golf, or some other athletic endeavor. Did he always enjoy baseball practice, or did he consider it a job, simply something that had to be done to stay on a ball club. Was he always looking for new ways to improve his performance? Did he get discouraged when he lost a game, or was hit hard? Did he ever read about the history of the game, the outstanding players, and what made them great?

When I was growing up in Michigan, I had certain chores to do, and when they were completed I headed for the baseball field. I was very fortunate in having a number of buddies who loved the game equally as well as myself. My love for the game has never faltered, and at times I am upset because people make changes in our national pastime that make no sense; artificial playing surfaces, designated hitters, a much smaller strike zone, and changes in the liveliness of the baseball.

My advice to any young player who does not fully enjoy and love the game is to forget about high level baseball. You might be able to play some high school ball games (but that too is questionable), but you will never succeed in professional baseball. In pro games I've played with such players and they are constantly in trouble with managers, coaches, and even fellow team members. A non caring, non hustling, disinterested ball player cannot hide on a ball field. Even the fans can spot such a player almost immediately.

As I have mentioned earlier, it takes great dedication to be a successful pitcher in this day and age. In the last twenty years, the mound has been lowered, and the baseball has been juiced up. The strike zone has been cut nearly 30%. You can no longer pitch inside as in the past, and hitters are now using hard wood bats that, in my judgment, should be illegal. The baseball literally jumps off of that type of wood, so much more so than the white ash wood that was in use in baseball for some eighty years. In addition, due to their tendency to splinter, they present a safety problem not only for the players on the field but also for the fans in the stands. What has been done for pitchers? Not a solitary thing.

The secret to successful pitching is getting ahead of the hitters in the count. In my day, hitters were aggressive, many times swinging at the first pitch, swinging at pitches a few inches high or low, or off the plate. Now they are "take" hitters, knowing that with the small strike zone if they wait long enough, the pitcher will be behind in the count and they can pick on a cripple, usually a nice fat fastball. In my day, pitchers would usually get a pitch a couple of inches high, low, or inside or outside, especially when the hitter had two strikes on him. The feeling being that the hitters should be protecting the plate and that quality of a pitch was too close to take. Not now – umpires will call that pitch a ball, even with that cut-down strike zone. Every big league umpire should be placed on the mound and made to throw fifty pitches into that tiny bit of space called the strike zone. They had best bring a sleeping bag with them for they will be there all night. In recent years, homeruns have skyrocketed, batting averages increased, walks are out of sight, and of course, the poor pitchers ERA's have jumped nearly 2 points. Because of the strike zone, pitchers are now throwing 100 pitches by the 5th or 6th inning. Fans watch as nearly every batter in the box runs up a $3 - 2$ count. Isn't that exciting. Games drag on as walks fill the air and a parade of relief pitchers amble in from the bullpen. Of course, when August rolls around those same relief pitchers are so arm weary they can hardly get the ball to the plate.

Baseball, for years and years, was set up with a balance between hitting and pitching. There is absolutely no balance today, for it is strictly a hitters market. Promising young pitchers are now left in the minor leagues because they cannot pinpoint the ball in the strike zone. You might have a great arm with a great curveball, but because of the smallness of the strike zone, that over-hand downer is useless. It's just too difficult to get that type of pitch in that reduced zone. So pitchers give up that great pitch and turn to a slider; less break, better chance for a strike.

The complete game is almost a thing of the past in professional baseball. That is a shameful situation for this great game. Anyone with an ounce of baseball knowledge knows that the best pitchers in the game are the starting pitchers. Starting pitchers always have had a better selection of pitches. In the past, they were much more durable. Rather than preparing for a couple of innings, or a single inning, they had to work themselves through the batting order a number of times. In spring training, they started preparing themselves for the task by building up their legs, and strengthening their arms. As the season started they went maybe 7 innings the first couple of starts, then right into 9 innings. In 1952, Bob Lemon of the Indians had 28 complete games and his ERA was 2.50. Warren Spahn averaged 22 complete games for 15 straight seasons. Complete games breed confidence, and they instill pride. How much pride is involved today when a pitcher goes 5 or 6 innings and then hands the ball to a reliever. Then he sits around for another four or five days before he repeats the process.

There is nothing in baseball harder on a pitcher's arm than coming in day after day from the bullpen. In my day, young pitchers were brought up as starters. Now they are put in the bullpen as if they all had rubber arms. Many will pitch in 60 – 70 games, throwing less than 100 innings. In middle relief, they will gain little if any recognition. Many will end up with sore arms due to the frequency of their warm-ups in the bullpen. A starting pitcher has several days between starts for the arm to rest, but for most relievers, the arm never rests.

In my day, most clubs used a four man rotation. Today, most use a five day turn-around. Yet, managers refuse to let a starting pitcher finish what he starts. Time after time they are lifted in the middle innings with a lead, only to get a no decision because the relief man blows the lead. I have seen modern day managers lift a starting pitcher when he's working on a shutout, even when he's struck out the side in his last inning, simply because he feels he has to use his bullpen. What total nonsense. No starting pitcher should be removed from a game when he is performing his duties in a winning manner. If he's getting hit hard; if he admits to being tired; if he's injured; those are legitimate reasons. However, to remove him and run in another pitcher who is already tired, has an era of 5 or 6, and never did have the natural stuff to be a starter, well, that's downright stupid.

What modern managers do not understand is that a good starting pitcher, a solid competitor, will throw his best stuff in the 7th, 8th, and 9th innings. I always had my best stuff in the late innings. With only 9, 6, or 3 outs to get, the good starter will reach back and get a little extra. In my own case, I can remember but one game in pro baseball when I lost a game in the 9th inning and that happened because my shortstop booted a ground ball with the winning run on third base. Years ago, managers stuck with their best in the late innings, and now and then they might blow a game in the ninth, but look at the blown games today. There are presently about three closers who are outstanding. The rest are far less talented than the starters on those teams.

Last evening, I watched a Yankee game and the starter was yanked in the 7th inning with a 3 – 0 lead. He had allowed but 2 hits the entire game. He wasn't tired, he was still throwing good stuff, but because he had two men on base, he was lifted. The relief pitcher came in and promptly gave up a 3 run homer. If that wasn't enough, he served up another homer to the next hitter. Now, doesn't that breed confidence in your starter!

Human nature is a rather funny thing. People never want to admit that they've made a mistake. Remember all those people jumping on the bandwagon for artificial turf for football and baseball fields? To hear them talk, it was the greatest thing since sliced bread. Why, natural turf was a thing of the past. It was years before they finally admitted that artificial turf was a total disaster. Baseballs were bouncing 20 feet into the air off the stuff, and player after player came up with all kinds of knee problems, burns, and muscle pulls. Many of the injuries ended promising careers.

Now we have the small strike zone. Whoever came up with that idea needs to be brought forth so he can attempt to explain the mess it's presently causing for some 300 or so big league pitchers.

With the return of a fair strike zone, baseball can once again start at the minor league levels and create starting pitchers as we did in the past. Pitchers would then take pride in their work, starting and finishing ball games. Games would contain some fine pitching performances, hitters would be more aggressive, and the fans could stop sitting through a dozen walks in about every game.

Time for a break, so stretch your legs, sip a little more of that cool drink, and then we'll move on to Chapter 6.

Chapter 6

They say everyone should swing to their waltz and I've had a number of them in my lifetime, but baseball has been my main passport to success, relaxation, and happiness. I owe a great deal to the game and I always try to do some special things as a repayment. I've held hundreds of clinics, operated summer baseball camps for some seventeen years, and talked at many sports banquets, and public schools, on the merits of this wonderful game. For more than twenty years, I traveled the highways and byways looking for professional talent so I might give a boy from Kentucky or Ohio, or elsewhere, a new start in life. I've signed a number of young men who came from families burdened with financial problems, and the young men, after reaching stardom, have built new homes for their parents, or rewarded them in various other ways. I well recall one young man in particular who went on to make a million dollars a year and spent 13 seasons in the big leagues.

There have been a number of occasions when I walked into a ballpark to look at one player and ended up liking another player who had a great deal more talent. Being an ex-pitcher, I was always looking for a good arm. If the clubs held infield practice, I checked out the arms from third base, shortstop, and the outfield positions. When I spotted a great arm, I checked on the player's batting average. If he was a weak hitter, there was always the chance of moving him to the mound. I have made the point earlier that any successful pitcher must start with a good strong arm.

So, my readers, remember my point. If you are a position player with a strong arm and have a great deal of difficulty with the bat, think about moving to the pitcher's mound. I played some third base and had a strong, accurate arm from that position. A number of times, I have signed former third basemen to pro contracts as pitchers.

Find a successful pitcher who can work with you on a breaking ball. Test your control out and see if your pitches are in or close to the strike zone. If you find that you're wild inside and outside, that can be easily corrected. If you're wild in the dirt and high out of the zone, that presents a much more serious problem. Seek help on a nice smooth fluid delivery that will help your control. I like third basemen because most have good size. Shortstops have some good arms, but most are of the smaller variety. It is well known that first and second basemen have the weaker arms in the infield.

Another point. Many big league clubs run tryout camps for free agent players. If you're 16 years of age or older, write the big league clubs and request a schedule and location of their camps. In my scouting days, I ran three camps each summer in all five states. Many of the boys were 16-18 years of age and playing on summer league teams. If they showed promise, I had them send me a baseball schedule and I did my best to see one of their games. If the boy was an upcoming junior or senior in high school, I requested that he send me his next year's school schedule.

At my tryout camps, we ran all players 60 yards in a straight line and timed them with a stop watch. Seven seconds flat was the average big league speed at that time. We threw all the outfielders, infielders, and catchers, looked at their fielding abilities, and then we held two regular games to look at the hitters and pitchers. The camps were held on Friday and Saturday, starting at 10 a.m. and ending around 3 p.m.

Some very important tips that will help you make a good impression. If you're a pitcher, make sure you have at least 3 or 4 days rest before reporting. You want to show the scouts a well-rested, good, live arm. Never attend a tryout camp with a sore arm. If, because of numbers, you were unable to throw in one of the games, make sure you throw on the sidelines for the scouts. If you do throw in a ballgame, make sure you use all of your pitches. Show good poise on the mound, solid control, and work quickly. Slow working pitchers drag the game along, irritate the scouts, and upset the position players. If you get the opportunity to hit or bunt, show the scouts that you've had some coaching and you're not an automatic out at the plate. Move quickly out to the mound and hustle off the field. Nothing impresses a scout more than hustle. If you play another position, well, ask the scout if you can work out in the infield or outfield.

Never leave a tryout camp early. Report early and be one of the last to leave. Although the scout and his assistant are not running an instructional camp, they will listen to any particular problem you might have with your pitching. If time allows, they will answer your questions and will take you aside to actually work on the problem. In my camps, I made time for such problems but you might attend a camp run by a scout with less patience. Attend as many camps by different big league clubs as possible. In time, you will find the ideal camp.

If you have a uniform available, wear it to camp; it is much more impressive than jeans and street clothes. Have a comfortable pair of spikes to run the 60 yards and pitch off the mound. Believe it or not, I have had kids report to camp and run the 60 yards in motorcycle boots!

If you have a favorite bat, bring it with you. As far as gloves are concerned, never attend a tryout camp with a worn out piece of leather, or a glove not fit for the position. Pitchers should have large gloves to cover their pitches well, and a second baseman, as an example, should have the smallest glove on the field so he can handle the throws on a double play without hesitation.

If you, as a pitcher, have the opportunity to pitch in a game, be sure to have a conversation with the boy behind the plate. After all, you probably have never met before and he has no knowledge of what you throw. Make sure you have a clear understanding of the signs.

As you enter the camp, you will be asked to fill out a player information card. As the scout will keep this card after the camp, be sure you print clearly and supply the correct information. In my own case, I kept a certain file for all my camp player information cards.

I have signed some fine ballplayers out of tryout camps. Although hard work, camps allowed me to see players unknown to me during my game coverage scouting. In one normal year, I probably saw 3,000 players in my camps.

Some more pointers for young pitchers. If you are a high school pitcher and have amassed some outstanding strikeout totals, send those stats to a big league ball club (send them to the scouting director) along with any articles you might have to verify your figures. As a scout and former pitcher, I was always interested in strikeout totals. Wins and losses meant very little, but strikeouts gave me a good picture of the boy's velocity. Again, everyone is impressed with a good arm. In high school, I had the strikeout numbers, and scouts attended my games from all over the country. By setting all the Michigan high school strikeout records, I received valuable press coverage. Any time you do something out of the ordinary in a game, or games, get copies of the newspaper article, and if your feat centers on strikeouts, make sure the article is placed in the proper hands.

I can well remember the first game I pitched that drew the attention of professional scouts. As a sophomore, I pitched the championship game of our two division league at Hastings, Michigan. I won 2-1 and had 25 strikeouts in a 9 inning contest. That was a state record and all the area newspapers picked up on the effort. By the time I started pitching in my junior year, I had heard from twelve different big league scouts. As a junior, I was invited to work out in Briggs Stadium for the Detroit Tigers. Again, strikeouts can open many doors.

Some more pointers. We have but one arm to throw a baseball with at any amount of velocity. The arm was not put on the human body to throw a baseball, so supreme care must be taken to prevent injury. It is a great temptation wanting to throw curveballs at an early age. It was for me, and it is for most young pitchers. By the age of 15 years, know how to grip and throw a curveball or slider, but use the pitch very sparingly. Know how to use your entire body, your hips, your back, your shoulders, your legs, to take the pressure off your arm and elbow. It is the breaking of the wrist that causes the exchange of pressure to the elbow and the shoulder. If we, as pitchers, could throw nothing but fastballs during a contest, we would seldom ever have a sore arm. So, be very careful when you're 16 and limit the breaking pitch to a few deliveries per game. Work on your velocity, the movement of your fastball, and perfect your control. There will be coaches asking you to throw a larger number of breaking pitches but you must stand fast and protect your arm. There is no hurry in securing a curveball or slider. A talented pitching coach can teach the pitch in a few outings.

Another important point. Have a routine of conditioning after throwing a ballgame. The best healer for a sore or stiff arm is rest. The day after I pitched a ballgame, I had some soreness and stiffness, so I never picked up a baseball for at least one day and at times, two.

Do some running and let the arm and shoulder muscles rest. I've been around some pitching coaches who preached doing some throwing even though there was some soreness in the forearm, or between the elbow and the shoulder. Bad advice and I never listened to a word of it. One throw at the wrong moment can end a promising career.

I knew from early in my career that I could never be a relief pitcher. My arm never allowed me to throw two days in a row. However, with four days rest, I could throw nine or more innings and still have good stuff in the last inning. My professional managers always used me as a starter and for that consideration, I will be forever grateful.

Another point. Do not complain to umpires when you're on the mound. I've known all sorts of umpires in amateur and professional baseball, some better than others at calling balls and strikes. I've always felt that, by giving them the benefit of the doubt, I prospered in the long run. Sure, they will miss a pitch now and then, they usually realize the mistake themselves, but by keeping quiet and never showing them up, you will get a pitch or two later in the game. I played for a certain manager in pro ball years ago who would never get on a home plate umpire and he detested managers who constantly yelled from the dugout about certain calls. No manager has that kind of eyesight he would mutter. He believed in fairness, and in my judgment, his integrity added to his stature.

One more point. Never cheat on the game. The game of baseball is bigger than any player, any team, or any league. I have known pitchers who work for a couple of innings to cover the rubber with dirt and then place their heel against the front of the rubber to gain a foot on a two strike pitch. I've known pitchers to scuff and cut the baseball to gain an advantage. When they bragged of their cleverness, I simply walked away. If you cannot retire certain hitters, take your medicine and pitch on the up and up. Prepare yourself a little better, make some outstanding pitches, and those same troublesome hitters will seem quite ordinary.

Time for a break. Just think how much you've learned my young pitchers; and there's much more to come. Chapter 7 is just ahead.

Beardslee Fans 26 As Regular Season Finishes

(Special to the Enquirer and News)

VERMONTVILLE—Ken Beardslee and his Vermontville high school baseball team closed out the 1949 season yesterday by scoring a nine-inning 3 to 2 victory over Holt in a non-league affair.

Beardslee, the much sought-after senior righthander, not only pitched his team to victory but was "in" on all the runs scored by Vermontville.

Beardslee hurled five-hit ball yesterday and got all but one of the Holt batters via the strikeout route, racking up 26 more strikeouts to his already fine record. Ken walked only one batter.

Beardslee was safe on an error as Ron Mull came in with the first run in the opening inning and he singled in the fourth and came home on Al Mix's triple. In the ninth, Jack Cranson singled and Beardslee pounded out a triple to win the game.

Holt's two runs came in the fourth and sixth with a man singling in each frame, stealing second and third and coming home on hits.

The line score:

```
                       R  H  E
Holt  ........ 000 101 000—2  5  2
Vermontville . 100 100 001—3  5  4
```

Green and DePuew; Beardslee and Mull.

Above: Ken as he looked in high school.

Above: Ken Beardslee is shown here fifty years ago during his pro debut with the Yankees' farm team in Newark, Ohio. At Vermontville, Beardslee set national records for no-hitters and strikeouts that still stand. By 1956, his career was done, but he made a name for himself as a Pittsburgh Pirates scout.

Above: The author with Dizzy Dean, the Hall of Fame St. Louis Cardinal right-hander.

Above: Ken, holding the Alabama/Florida Trophy alongside General Hendrickson, Manager Bradley, and Colonel Miller at Camp Rucker, Alabama. The author pitched and won six games in a row during the championship run.

**Above: The author with his first pro manager,
Jim McLeod.**

**Above: The author with Charlie Maxwell, former
outfielder for the Detroit Tigers.**

Left: Ken, with Doug Melvin, General Manager of the Milwaukee Brewers.

Below: The author with Terry Collins, former manager of the Houston Astros and the California Angels.

Chapter 7

For just a single chapter I would like to mention the importance of young players playing the proper position. For years when I was scouting, I was frustrated by the sight of high school players being placed at positions where their talent was completely wasted. Many a time, I have had to ask a coach to play a boy at another position so I might evaluate his professional potential.

Let's start with the infield. First, arrange the positions into two separate divisions. Requirements for playing shortstop and second are totally different than those at first and third. At shortstop, the player must have a strong arm, have very quick feet, soft hands, and be an adequate hitter. Most are very agile and have great body control, for they must cover a great deal of area. At second base, the player must have all the talents I have mentioned for the shortstop position, except the strong arm. His throws are shorter and most will come from a different angle. Many second basemen seldom come over the top with a throw. By throwing side arm, they can get rid of the ball a little quicker, especially while making the double play. At third base, the player must have a strong arm, be very quick on the first step, and here the throws will be over the top or high three quarter. However, there are throws that demand a much different angle. He must be able to go to his left toward the hole and make that type of throw; then there's the topped ball which he must charge and throw off his left foot. As a hitter, he must have more power than the middle infielders. I will say, in recent years, the shortstop position has produced players with good power but for years this was not the case. At first base and at third, running speed is not as important as at shortstop and second. The talented first baseman must have good hands, an adequate but not great arm (his longest throw will be to third base and that throw is seldom made), and he must have some power in his bat. The tall, left-handed first baseman is ideal.

The catching position. Most catchers have some good size for it's a position that takes a beating to all parts of the body. When selecting a boy for catching, look at the strength in his hands and in his forearms. He must have a strong arm to throw out fast base runners. Does he enjoy the position? It's the toughest position physically on the field and unless you love getting behind the plate, the wear and tear will soon discourage the best of athletes. If a catcher can handle pitchers and be great on defense, his hitting can be below average. There are catchers in the big leagues keeping their position and hitting 225 or a little better.

The outfield. You cannot hide a poor arm in the outfield. Every club will run on such a player. The weakest arm, however, is usually put in left field for his throws are shorter. The best arm goes to the right fielder for he has to make that long throw to third base. The center fielder should also have a strong arm. All outfielders should have some power but there are some exceptions. At times, you will find an outfielder with great running speed endowed with the ability to line the ball into the gaps. A solid outfielder has the talent to come in, or go straight back on a ball. If he has a great arm, base runners will respect that part of his game and will think twice about taking an extra base.

Believe it or not, while scouting high school ball players, I have seen left-handers playing shortstop, or second base. Unless there are no other players available, that type of positioning is a total waste of everybody's time.

On a positive note, all coaches should be aware of a strong arm. I like to use as an example the major league career of one Bob Lemon, the former great pitcher of the Cleveland Indians. Bob played four years for the tribe as a third baseman and outfielder, then someone got the bright idea to move him to the mound. During the next thirteen years, he won a total of 207 games while losing but 128. Seven different seasons he won more than 20 games and in 1976 was voted into the Baseball Hall of Fame. That's quite a switch!

Now let's move on to another very important pointer on the journey to becoming a winning pitcher.

During my active career, I always felt that the first hitter up in the inning was the most important. Remember, if the first hitter reaches base, you are then pitching from the stretch position. It was no secret to me that I had far better velocity from the windup than from the stretch. The reason being, with a windup a pitcher can use more leg kick, more body turn, and does not have to hurry his delivery. Another important factor is the point of your concentration. If you retire the first hitter in the inning, you are then able to devote 100% of your concentration upon the second hitter. However, if that first hitter reaches, you must give the base runner a portion of that concentration. Unless you are fortunate enough to have your infielders turn a double play, you probably will spend the entire inning pitching from the less than desired stretch position. A base on balls or hit with two outs and nobody on base seldom hurts a pitcher, but that first hitter reaching can be a killer. When I was pitching, I really bore down on that first hitter making sure I got ahead in the count and forcing him to hit the ball some place. If I got lucky with a strikeout, so much the better. There are far too many base on balls these days. Anytime you walk a hitter you've probably thrown from 6-8 pitches, then mix that pitch count along with a couple of 3-2 counts, plus a hit or so and you've already thrown more than twenty pitches your first inning. If that is your routine, you will never last past the 5th or 6th inning in any of your starts. I do not have the percentages before me, but I would wager that probably half of those first hitter walks eventually score.

It is a known fact that there are more runs scored in the first inning than any other. You must be prepared to throw strikes right from the start of any contest. How sharp must you be? Remember the lead-off man usually has the best eye in the line-up. Walk him and you have a speedy runner to worry about. Then, of course, you must face a tough second place hitter who can hit and run. After him, you have the meat of the line-up in the 3rd and 4th place hitters. The message is clear; you can win or you can lose depending on how well you handle that first hitter.

Another important point to remember. Do you have any idea how many pitches you can save yourself in a nine inning game by getting that first pitch in for a strike? Knowing that I had good control, many hitters would swing at the first pitch and make outs. Even if they took the strike, they then would be in the hole in the count and did not dare take another strike. Making the hitter use his bat can be a great advantage for any pitcher. By throwing first pitch strikes, his pitch count during those crucial seventh, eighth, and ninth innings will be lowered considerably. What a blessing it is to be able to throw strikes. How difficult is the game for the pitcher who is always running up 3-2 counts.

There is an old saying in golf that there are two things in life that never last. Dogs chasing cars, and pro's putting for pars. Pitchers walking hitters will never last either.

Another pointer. Make sure your catcher gives you a full faced target. What I mean by full faced is simply what it implies. Make sure his mitt face is completely visible to you when you're making your delivery. Some catchers get a little lazy and will drop the top portion of their mitt, thus giving you only half a target. Remember, you're not throwing at anything but the catcher's mitt, so make sure it's full faced, and where you want to throw your pitch. Another pointer. I always took my warm-up pitches between innings very seriously. I never lobbed the pitches to the catcher, rather after the first warm-up throw, I concentrated on throwing a couple of fastballs in the strike zone, and then followed with a couple of breaking pitches. When the hitter came to the plate, I felt I was ready to give him my best stuff, in the strike zone.

I have at times warmed up in the bullpen before a game and realized that my curveball was not as sharp as usual. In most cases, it came around as the innings rolled by, but I used it sparingly in the first few innings. In such cases, you must use all your ingenuity and experience to get you through those early innings. A great pitcher is one who can manage to win without his best stuff. If you do not have your best fastball early on, then you must go to your breaking pitches and change of speed deliveries. Show them your fastball, but make sure it's around the plate, not in a great hitting area.

I once pitched a ballgame while in the military service against Fort Benning, Georgia, a fine hitting ball club. I did not have my curveball, for I had developed a blister on my index finger. Instead, I stuck with my good velocity fastball and straight change. I won the game 8-0, striking out but a single hitter.

I am convinced that any pitcher with a good, strong arm, the willingness to learn, having an inventive imagination, and a sound work foundation, can win four games for every one he loses. Yes, with a good ball club, he might even win at a five or six to one ratio. But to do so he must master not only the obvious hurdles, he must come up with solutions to all the smaller obstacles. During a full season, it is amazing how many of these smaller problems surface. If you ignore them, they will literally eat into your win total making you a 500 pitcher, or even worse by season's end.

It is usually considered a long, tedious process to acquire fame, to win national recognition for worthy endeavor. But, in reality, it can be a great adventure, a journey of learning, and of course upon completion it carries a monumental sense of pride. Baseball offers such recognition, if the player is conscious of his obligations.

As a player, I kept score of battles won and lost; checked triumphs against disappointments; always resisted disillusionments; and my dreams and fantasies were always in bloom. I chose to keep a path leading everywhere.

So, my young pitchers, have a sublime creed in your work, a creed that will suffice for all occasions and matters that might impede your progress, a creed of dedication that will carry you steadily onward, and never once desert you.

Now, let's once again take a brief break, preparing ourselves for all of the little gems in chapter 8.

Chapter 8

I hope all of you young pitching hopefuls will pay close attention to what I have to say in this chapter. The ability to recognize and correct one's own mistakes is the mark of a true champion. The pitcher who purposely excuses himself for his errors, instead of trying to eliminate them, seldom rises above mediocrity.

There's the pitcher who always seems to have an alibi or excuse for his shortcomings. I am reminded of the golfer who noted, "I don't think I will ever excel in this game. You have to beat the sun, the wind, the rough, the rules committee, the gallery, the spike marks when I'm putting, as well as my opponent. I don't think I'll ever win a match."

I have heard pitchers moan after giving up a homerun in a tight contest, "How lucky can a hitter be? I made a perfect pitch, he swung off-balance, and hit it over the fence." Well, if it was a perfect pitch, how come it traveled 430 feet! A true champion is first to place the blame upon himself when he knows that is where it belongs. The saddest part about the alibi is that nobody believes it except the one who makes it up, and he believes it completely. I once knew a pitcher who could not get past the 7th inning. It seemed every game he pitched, he threw well until the last quarter and then he always ran into trouble. I knew I could help him, so during a game when neither of us was pitching, I asked him outright about his late game problems. With a straight face he said, "Oh, it's the mound you know. By the 7th inning I've dug a rather deep hole where my left foot comes down. I try to smooth the spot out, but I never can get it back where it was in the early innings. It affects my control and I start getting behind the hitters and before you know it, I've given up two or three runs." He just shook his head and resigned himself to his ghastly fate.

I resolved to end this, so I told him, "You're making excuses, Frank, and the mound has absolutely nothing to do with your late inning failures." I got up from the bench and started to leave but before departing, I shot back, "I'll be around if you want to talk about it." As I walked away, I could hear him sputtering.

Frank went on another two games, blowing up in both of them. We went on the road the next day and one afternoon I was sitting in the hotel lobby when Frank grabbed a seat beside me. I could tell he wanted to talk. "Ok, know it all. What's my problem?"

I explained I certainly did not know it all, but I did know why he was wild in the late innings. I told him he was wild because his legs were not in shape. I reminded him that I ran for 45 minutes the day after I pitched and he ran for 10. I also explained that when a pitcher's legs start to go in the late innings, the pitches are usually high and outside to a left-handed hitter (from a right-handed pitcher).

It's almost automatic and easy to spot from the bench. I asked him, "Have you ever paid attention to my pitches late in a game?" "Not really," was his reply. "Well, Frank," I answered, "I can tell you I seldom ever walk a hitter period, but in the late innings the results are no different than in the first three innings. It's no mystery, many other winning pitchers get the same results because they've built up their legs for the long haul." I told him I knew he did not have a chronic control problem, which was true. Frank looked a hole into me, or so it seemed, and then without a word he got up and left.

For the rest of the season, to my memory, he got 10 or 12 starts. During the first couple, he showed little progress but as the season wore on, he started going a little farther into each game. I do know that he finished several contests before he went home. Several times, when the rotation allowed, he completed his running with me alongside. He forgot all about making excuses and admitted to his own mistakes.

The lesson here is obvious. Stop telling yourself that outside circumstances are keeping you from being a big time winner. The trouble with the alibi game is that it's too easy. Anyone can explain a licking on the mound by blaming it on the hitters, the umpires, the defense, and a host of other things. It takes a real man to blame a defeat on himself.

How easy it would have been for me to use the old "double barreled alibi"; I can't concentrate on pitching because sometimes during the course of the game a great story pops into my head and you certainly cannot retire a good hitter when you're thinking about writing. Or, I cannot write that great story or poem for it seems about the time I get this great idea at the typewriter, I dream about being on the mound and pitching a no-hitter. See how easy the alibi game can be played?

In this chapter, I want to take some space to mention temper, a mood one could call expansive, irritable. I have seen pitchers come into the dugout after a bad inning and literally tear the place apart, throwing gloves, bats, and dismantling the water cooler. Of course, when they went back out for the next inning, they were totally useless. Composure under stress is a winner in any profession. In the pitching game, there will be bad innings, sometimes caused by the pitcher himself, and at other times caused by one's own teammates. Now and then, an umpire will have an off day or evening. It is all a part of the game that one must accept and move on. Baseball is not a game of total perfection. It is played by humans, umpired by humans, and we all know humans make mistakes. The beauty of the game lies in its unpredictability. How boring it would be if we knew in advance exactly what the next play would bring. Once a pitcher has accepted this master plan he can handle his emotions in a less stressful manner.

Allow me to test my memory once again. One evening, I was pitching a game in the Carolina League against Greensboro. Going into the ninth inning, I held a 2-1 advantage. I had runners on second and third with two outs when the hitter hit an ordinary ground ball to our shortstop. Perhaps the ball took a bad bounce, and then maybe he took his eye off the ball. Regardless, the ball went between his legs and both runs scored. I lost the game. I was bitterly disappointed. In the clubhouse, I found the infielder before his locker, his head in his hands. We were the best of friends and I knew the feeling he had at that moment. I sat down in the next locker and we talked for maybe fifteen minutes. I reminded him of all the games in which he had saved me hits and runs. I explained the human factor to him and how we are all a part of that formula. In due time, he forgot about his error and he played his usual fine game at shortstop.

As a pitcher, I've never tried to get too high, or two low, emotion-wise. Stay on an even keel.

A loss of temper means a poor decision is about to happen. Take the hitter as an example. He feels he received a bad call from the umpire, so he jaws at him before walking back to the dugout. What has he accomplished? Absolutely nothing. Before he reaches the dugout he could be removed from the game by the umpire. If he stays in the game and bats again in the next few innings, he is sure to be remembered by the umpire and his chances of getting close pitches are slim at best. He is still upset by the earlier call and it's sure to affect his plate performance for the rest of the contest. All of these possibilities due to the fact that he lost his temper.

Remember you can be a great competitor without losing your temper. In my mind, a solid competitor always battles the opposition and keeps his emotions under control. The great Walter Johnson, Hall of Fame pitcher for the Washington Senators, was a fine example. He won 416 games for a sub par team and was known as the gentlest, most reserved, and best loved player of his time.

Now, I shall shift gears and bring forth another important pointer that could win you a number of games during your career.

All during my days on the mound, I was regarded as a fast working pitcher. I have had so many position players come up to me and say, "Ken, I so enjoy playing behind you because you work so quickly."

I know all of you readers have watched slow working pitchers either at the park or on TV. First these pitchers must fool around with the uniform, the cap, the trousers, then makes a couple of trips to the rosin bag, and then they stare at the catcher for what it seems a number of seconds before getting the proper sign. After he delivers the pitch and receives the ball back from the catcher, he must circle the mound and then repeat the entire process. In the meantime, the infielders are up on their toes, gloves out in front of their bodies, resting just above the surface, all waiting for that pitch that never seems to develop. Same situation with the outfielders, and the poor catcher has been squatting so long he starts to have leg cramps. The umpire, of course, is fuming. It's been a hot day and he's thinking about that cold drink after the game.

Here's the correct procedure. Once you receive the ball back from the catcher or umpire, you immediately return to the rubber. You get your sign and you deliver the pitch. I always had an agreement with my catcher that I wanted him to give me the sign as soon as possible. I was not going to walk around the mound or do all the other silly things that most of the pitchers were doing. I have seen some pitchers from the stretch position raise their arms over their heads and then bring those arms down to the set position like an elevator slowly descending from the 30th floor.

In short, all the position players behind you perform so much better, are so much more alert, and spend much less time on the field when you work quickly on the mound. None of the players, umpires, or fans are looking forward to a game that lasts for four hours. Every manager that I ever played for was upset with slow working pitchers.

Even though we love game conditions, we must always strive to eliminate time on the field. Pitchers must work to lower their pitch count, to cut back on the number of base on balls, and to speed up their actions on the mound. If the contest is a low scoring game, let's say 2-1 or 3-2, there is no reason why two fast working pitchers cannot complete the game in a little over two hours.

Now, take a break and then we'll move on to the next chapter.

Chapter 9

In addition to my love for baseball, I have a second passion and that is for reading and writing. While composing a story or some poetry, I experience the same golden feeling that I have always felt when walking onto a baseball field. I am sure there are many stories of young lads who had to work at an early age when others their age reveled in the stories which make childhood the golden age of dreams, of heroes and magic kingdoms. Then they grew up and some found great wealth, built fine libraries, filled with the world's greatest stories. Their old age was rich with the good fellowship that reading can bring. Now, they thought, we will make up for the lost dreams of our youth. Now we will read the legends, the great childhood adventure books, the tales and songs that gladden our hearts. They then opened those glorious books but a strange thing happened; the magic was gone. How true it is that the inspiring stories we read as children remain with us as rich, inspiring memories for the remainder of our lives. If we miss them in youth, their magic is gone forever.

The same may be said about growing up with baseball. When I was growing up, I had the good fortune of having a baseball field right at my doorstep. With some cracked bats, a well worn baseball, and some gloves more than a bit past their prime, we would choose up sides and have a game without umpires, but a contest that contained all sorts of exciting moments. I can still remember the names of most of those players and of course all the games that I later played with them in high school. As I have mentioned earlier, I have pitched ballgames all over this country, and in several other countries, but none that I enjoyed more than those pick-up games when I was growing up in Michigan.

Baseball is much more than just a game, it's a national tradition, and for those who appreciate its great values, its honesty, its building of character qualities, it is apple pie with all the trimmings. Take, for instance, the umpires. Until recently, most were vastly underpaid and for years they have remained incorruptible while others, even in the government, have learned to wink at payola. They are berated by players and managers, and fans feel justified in shouting all sorts of cruel indignities their way. Even the sportswriters will rejoice when they are outwitted. They will call games off when great gate receipts may be lost, and they will toss from the field players whose very presence has lured a third of the customers. What is it that lures former players and former managers into a profession where he must crouch behind the catcher on a hot July afternoon during the course of a 12 inning game? What brings him to a profession where he must spend most of the season by himself, free from the association of many of the great players whom he admires and respects? One thing we know for sure; their immunity to temptation. No professional umpire has ever been accused of accepting a bribe. Their honesty, their loyalty to fair play, stems from their great love for the game. They can well recall their youthful days on a dirt infield either in the large city, or in a small town somewhere out in the heartland of this country. When they have the duty of rubbing up the glossy new balls before a professional game they are once again back in their youth, holding a brand new baseball for the first time, perhaps as a birthday or Christmas present.

My first memories of the game go back to the afternoons when I would sit on the floor in front of the family radio and listen to the golden tones of Harry Heilmann, the accomplished Detroit Tiger announcer. Harry had been a great outfielder for the Tigers back when Ty Cobb was making headlines with all his daring feats. With Heilmann at the mike, I could almost feel as though I was sitting right next to the dugout watching all of those talented players perform on the green grass of Briggs Stadium. Speaking of the green grass of the ballpark, I can well remember walking from the cement of the city into that sea of greenery and thinking why it's just like back home in Eaton County, gazing out over a couple of acres of prime pasture land.

What a fan I was of this glorious game. Today I hear people talk about the loyalty of the Chicago Cub's fans, but when I was playing in the minor leagues, I played for a number of teams where the fans were equally as loyal. Sometimes those fans would do such marvelous things for the players. They would walk into the clubhouse with chewing gum, candy bars, soft drinks, or even chewing tobacco for a player or two, and all they wanted in return was a thank you. I've had fans before my locker asking if they could shine up my baseball spikes.

When I played, the players, while at home, would stay at a small apartment near the ballpark. It was usually one room with a bed, a chair or two, and maybe a desk. The family owning the house would allow you to use the kitchen, and now and then they would invite you to sit down with them and enjoy a special dinner. In the afternoon, if they were going uptown, they would take you along, and many a time I joined these wonderful fans in a nice drive through the countryside. At times, I've had a landlady gather up my laundry and, without a word, do it all up nicely and lay it out on the bed. What kind and gracious fans. I could not close this paragraph without mentioning one other kindness they performed. If a player was a little short before payday, these fans were always there with a few extra bucks.

Players should always remember their obligations to the fans. They are in the stands showing their support, rain or shine. I can well remember whenever I had two strikes on a hitter, they would rise from their seats and with shouts I could not help but hear, encourage me to record another strikeout. Whenever I finished a successful inning at home, I always tipped my cap to the fans as I walked into the dugout. A small gesture, but I wanted to let them know I appreciated their support. All players should remember that they are role models, like it or not, and all that you do while on or off the field reflects on your character. Your actions are being watched by fans of all ages, including kids, perhaps attending a game for the first time, and your first impression is most important for it can never be reversed.

I have played on clubs where a player or two would not sign an autograph. The word spread like wildfire and those players never received the kindness and respect from the fans as the rest of the team members. I have been on clubs where a player or two would refuse to do acts of community service and those players were likewise scorned by most of the fans. I always made myself available for baseball clinics during the course of the season, and the fans always responded in a positive manner.

In Norfolk, Virginia, when I was pitching in the Piedmont League, I met a special fan who always sat directly behind our dugout. A few years ago, in a book entitled, **RHYMES FOR ALL TIMES** (my first published book of poetry), I included a poem titled, **BEN**. I wrote those verses one day after talking by phone with some very special fans from that area. In the past few years, I have had more public response to that poem than any other selection in the book. It seems to me that this is the proper chapter to include the verses in this book.

BEN

When I was in the Piedmont League
Pitching for the Yank's
I dreamed of Yankee Stadium
Of rising through the ranks.

That year I found a special friend
A man of warmth and grace
A man who always seemed to have
A smile upon his face.

He owned a season ticket pass
And always dressed the same
A tailored suit, white shirt, and tie,
That's how he always came.

He wore upon his snow-white hair
A Yankee baseball cap
He always bought a scorecard
And placed it on his lap.

I called him by his first name, Ben,
That's all I ever knew
We often talked about the game
That's how our friendship grew.

His voice was but a whisper
So gentle in its tone
To games he rode a city bus
And always came alone.

He told me he had seen the best
In one's that made this stop
He always said I had the stuff
To make it to the top.

He sat in section twenty-four
His seat was number eight
He never caught an early bus
When games were dull or late.

He always thought of baseball
In terms of joy and pride
With his hand he gave a little wave
When I retired the side.

One night while drinking water
I glanced above my cup
And saw that Ben was absent
His seat was folded up.

I learned that Ben had taken ill
That he had died that day
That he was coming to the park
When he passed away.

My last six starts at Norfolk
Were wins, I couldn't be beat
And with each win, I tipped my cap,
To Ben, there in his seat.

Ben was very special, he touched my heart and, like so many fans, his life revolved around baseball. Like the first Robin of spring, the first golden daffodil after winter, for Ben and all others, baseball was and continues to be the true beginning of another year. It's exciting, it's rewarding, it's uplifting, and it thrills the heart. It's opening day at Wrigley field.

Now let's get ready for chapter 10.

Chapter 10

Back to my pitching pointers. When I first entered professional baseball at the age of eighteen years, I searched for articles representing the rarest thoughts of the best known pitchers of the day. Many of their thoughts were fugitives, which for years had strayed in many directions before they were enclosed between a magazine's cover. I can well remember one article by a very successful pitcher on the subject of not repeating your mistakes.

I have seen so many pitchers dig themselves into a hole by not working on the many points of winning pitching that I have stated in this book. All of you young pitchers, when you find yourself in a hole, **STOP DIGGING**. Turn around, crawl out of the hole, and start all over again. We have all made mistakes in baseball, and in life, and the secret to improvement is not to repeat those mistakes. I have seen pitchers serve up a fastball to a hitter with a very quick bat and he promptly deposited it about 400 feet in the stands. Three innings later, that same pitcher gave that hitter the same pitch, with the same results. Time after time, I've seen pitchers making the same fielding error, the same balk motion, giving up runs in the first inning, walking the lead-off man in an inning, and the list goes on and on and on. When you make a mistake as a pitcher, make a mental and paper note, and file it away in your memory bank. What an asset it is for a pitcher to have a sharp memory. If you are playing in a league where you face the same hitters time and time again, remember those hitters you face, remember what pitches they like, and the ones they take because they have no success in swinging at them. Remember the flat footed ones that never stride, and the ones with the wide stride that you can change speeds on. If they're good fastball hitters, give them something else.

I would say that 80% of the homeruns that Sammy Sosa hits are from fastballs, either in the middle of the plate or to the outside portion of the plate. When he hits a good breaking pitch, it is usually at waist level. As a pitcher, you cannot give him those types of pitches to hit. Pitchers with a good live fastball should pitch him inside with the fastball, then go low and away with the breaking ball and their change. I'm not saying that this system is foolproof. Now and then he will hit good pitches, but he's not going to be hitting 65 homers per season off the pitches I have mentioned. That's why location is so important; that's why I mentioned earlier in the book about my keeping track of waist high swings. Making Sosa go down for the breaking pitches and changes, and raising his hands a little on the fastball inside, gives the pitcher an advantage. There are a number of players who upper-cut the baseball. One of the St. Louis Cardinal outfielders loves the ball waist high or a little lower (Edmonds). He's a good hitter but he has trouble with the high fastball. However, I've seen pitchers throw pitch after pitch right in his wheel house. Again, mistake after mistake.

In 1955, I pitched an entire season and allowed five homeruns. Oh, I gave up singles, some doubles, and maybe a triple or two, but I kept the ball in the ballpark. In almost all instances, it takes a mistake by the pitcher for a hitter to hit the ball 360-400 feet. Ted Williams made the statement that most pitchers are dumb. They kept pitching him in the wrong areas. In his book, **THE SCIENCE OF HITTING**, Ted has a chart showing where in the strike zone he hit the best. From four inches above the waist to four inches below the waist he figures he hit around 360! On knee high pitches to the outside corner, he states around 250! Even the best hitter in baseball had some troubles when a smart pitcher with good stuff had good location.

Although in many of these chapters I've discussed professional pitchers, I want to make it clear that almost all of my tips will make you a winner at the college and the high school level. Always be around the plate with your pitches, for I would wager that half of all strikeouts occur with pitches out of the strike zone. I know from experience that most third strikes I got were on high fastballs that hitters chased, or on curveballs from 3-6 inches off the corner. One must realize that any hitter is very anxious with only one strike left. Unless you have a 3-2 count, why give him a pitch in the strike zone? As I mentioned in an earlier chapter, never waste a pitch far out of the strike zone. Make the pitch close, a few inches below the knees, high at the letters, or a little off the corners. High school hitters seldom have a great eye at the plate and high school umpires will give you many pitches that are close.

Deception is very important for pitchers but not at the high school level. In high class college leagues, and in any pro circuit, hitters think timing, timing, timing; no swing should be too quick or too late. That's when the deception pays off for a well prepared pitcher. Take a little off the fastball, vary the speed of the curveball, just enough to upset the hitter's timing.

I have, at times, speeded up my wind-up for a pitch or two, and then returned to a normal speed to confuse a hitter and disrupt his timing. I have paused a bit longer in my stretch position to make the hitter wait a little longer, and make a base runner pause a few more seconds in his lead. Any time you throw a certain pitch to set up the next pitch, you are attempting to deceive the hitter. Look up deceptive in your dictionary and it reads, "Capable of being mistaken for something else." That's exactly what you're doing when you change speeds on your pitches, and when you fail to fall into a set pattern.

Another pointer. Never let up on a 3-0 pitch to a good hitter. Never aim the ball to get a strike. I always put some heat on that 3-0 pitch, for many times a good hitter will swing at that pitch hoping to get a real cripple. How many homeruns have I seen given up on a 3-0 count? From other pitchers a great many. I never experienced the embarrassment.

Ted Williams said that hitting is 50% from the neck up. Believe me, pitching is no different. Most hitters, even Williams, do not like to swing at the first pitch. They want to see if you have that little extra on your fastball, or that quick break on your curveball. But, by taking that first pitch for a strike, the advantage goes to the pitcher. So, please my young friends, make sure that first pitch is not a ball.

As I've mentioned earlier, a bad habit on the baseball field cannot be hidden. When Ted Williams was managing the Washington Senators, he had a homerun hitter in his line-up by the name of Frank Howard. Frank could hit the baseball 500 feet but never knew the strike zone and swung at far too many pitches out of the zone. Williams, who loved hunting, was in Africa one winter and a missionary came up to him and asked, "Is Frank Howard still swinging from the heels at those bad pitches?" If missionaries in

Nairobi had that information, why didn't American League pitchers? In 1968, '69, and '70, Frank Howard hit a total of 176 homeruns and averaged a fine 284 batting average. As Williams noted, there were a great many dumb pitchers out there on the mound.

I have signed some pitchers who made me mighty proud. One of those was a right-hander from Bowling Green University, Doug Bair. I liked him from the first game I saw him pitch against Western Michigan University. He had great movement on his fastball and he showed me a high three quarter curveball that gave just about all hitters a rough time. Doug was highly intelligent and a hard worker. He spent a little time in the minors and then went right up to the big leagues where he stayed for many seasons. He was a thinking pitcher and I saw a great deal of myself in his makeup.

Each year, when I speak at sport gatherings, youngsters come up to me and ask if they should attend a junior college, or perhaps a small college, rather than take the chance of attending a university and receiving limited playing time. Of course, the education considerations are the top priority, but from the baseball standpoint, I always make a single point. Go where you have a chance to play on a regular basis. Only from playing on a game to game schedule can you improve, or be observed by a professional scout. All during my twenty years of scouting I covered the small colleges as completely as I covered the Universities. Many fine prospects have been signed from junior colleges. Other youngsters have asked, "Do I have a chance coming from a small high school?" When I played, more than half of the high school players came from towns, not cities. Vern Ruhle, now a big league pitching coach, came from Coleman, Michigan; Jerry Lynch, a fine hitter for years in the big leagues, came from Munger, Michigan; Phil Regan, a great reliever, came from Wayland, Michigan; Dick Pole, a fine pitcher and now a big league pitching coach, came from Trout Creek, Michigan, and the list goes on and on. If you have the talent, the scouts will see you.

Let's shift gears a little and discuss Little League baseball. All over this country, we have thousands of people giving their time and efforts for that organization. When I was growing up, I never had the chance to play in the many youth leagues we have at present. There are many positive things to be said about Little League baseball, but there are also a great many negative aspects to the set up. I am a firm believer in kids having fun with the game at that age. With me, that's first priority. I heard a stat the other day from a very reliable source and though it did not surprise me, it was discouraging to say the least. In a nationwide poll, it was discovered that by the age of thirteen years, half of the youngsters that have participated in youth league baseball have dropped out of the game, completely burned out. In my judgment, there are far too many games, too much attention placed on winning, and too many youngsters sitting on the benches.

Years ago, I believe I was fortunate in going to the baseball field and playing a game of so called "work up", where we played all positions, hardly ever kept score, and simply had a grand old time. We practiced a great deal more than present youth leaguers. There was absolutely no pressure on any of us in those days. There was not a coach standing over us and shouting, or parents getting out of hand in the stands. I know I would never want to change that set up for what many youngsters participate in today.

When baseball proves to no longer be fun, the young player will turn to another sport, perhaps golf, where he can take his clubs and just roam the fairways, without pressure, simply having a wonderful time. There is a great deal of time later on for more games, more pressure, more talk of winning, but kids need to be kids, enjoying our wonderful game as free as birds on the wing, learning from their own experiences, and loving every minute of it.

With that, I too will take a break and return for chapter 11.

Chapter 11

One of the main reasons for the popularity of baseball for more than 100 years has to be due to the fact that players of all sizes have the opportunity to excel at the game. In basketball at high level play, almost all players have great height and have some speed. In football, almost all players must have good size. But in baseball, we have the speedy and small second baseman; the fleet-footed center fielder; the slower and more heavily set catcher; the tall slender first baseman; and of course pitchers can come in just about any size. I've known five foot seven inch pitchers who were big winners; on the other hand, we've all seen six foot four or six foot seven inch pitchers who were very talented. Which brings me to the main subject matter of this chapter.

All through the years that I was scouting, and even today to a lesser degree, I have received letters from parents and youngsters wanting to know if physical makeup was a factor for college or professional baseball.

Here might be a typical letter. "Mr. Beardslee, my son is a junior in high school. He throws right-handed, stands five foot eight, and tips the scales at 160 pounds. He throws around 86 miles per hour, has a good curveball, and throws a change up. He averaged 9 strikeouts per 7 inning game, and walks about 4 batters per game. Does he have a chance to play in a good college league, or even be considered by your club as a pro prospect?"

I, of course, would never write the boy off, or be interested in him as a pro prospect, unless I had the opportunity to see him perform on the field, but a letter like this one tells me a great many things about the boy's ability, and what he needs to work on.

So, all of you high school pitchers out there who fall into this boy's category, listen up.

At five foot eight inches, this boy, already a junior, probably will not be much larger when he graduates. So, he's going to be a small pitcher with a little bit better than average fastball for high school competition. With nine strikeouts per ballgame, it is obvious that he does not have two outstanding pitches. With four walks per game, he has much work to do on his control. So, unless he shows great improvement his senior year, he's going to have a tough time in good college baseball.

As I mentioned earlier in this book, I place great importance on strikeouts. A boy had to have from 12 – 15 strikeouts per seven inning game to really catch my eye. There is no reason why high school pitchers should be walking many hitters. The strike zone is much larger in high school and hitters swing at so many pitches that are out of the strike zone.

Any youngster with the stats of this boy needs to do the following. Get some movement on the fastball. Cut back on the number of walks. Throw as much as possible to build up arm strength (that's the only solution – no weights), and perhaps that strikeout ratio will improve next season.

Here might be another typical letter. "Dear Sir, I'm 17 years of age, six foot one inch, I weight 180 pounds. I just finished my junior year of high school and here are my stats. I pitched nine games, finished them all, a total of 63 innings. I allowed 45 hits, walked 18 batters, and struck out 120 hitters. Our league is a class B classification, not large, not small. Do I have a chance to pitch in the pros?"

Now, this boy catches my eye. He completes what he starts; he's around the plate with two walks every seven innings; and his strikeout ratio is far above average (innings). He has some good size and has another year of high school competition.

If you fall into this category, you're off to a good start towards a college or pro career. Now, how bad do you really want that career? You have an entire year to hone your skills. Take the pointers I have discussed in this book and the sky's the limit.

One more typical letter. "Dear Ken, I know I'm not a pro prospect but I want to improve to the point where I can pitch at a small college. I'm six feet tall and weight 175 pounds. I'm left-handed, and sometimes play first base when I'm not pitching. I hit rather well with a little power, but my running speed is not good. On the mound this year (junior), I pitched 54 innings, had 70 strikeouts (mostly with my curveball), and only walked 20 batters. What should I be working on now to make an impression next year?"

This would be my advice for all of you pitchers who fall into this category and throw left-handed. First of all, I want to mention that left-handers with some ability are in more demand than right-handers. If you have a good curveball, and can throw it for strikes, chances are there will always be a place for you to play in a good league. If I was a college coach, I would be interested in the above boy. He can hit some, that will help; he mentioned his curveball as his strikeout pitch so I'm to presume he's tough on left-handed hitters. His control is above average. What should he be working on? Everything I've talked about in this book. I do not agree that he's not a pro prospect. I have the feeling if I had the opportunity to work with this boy a few times, putting into action the tips I have mentioned in these chapters, he just might surprise everyone his senior year.

When you start with a decent arm, there's always hope that with hard work, some very sound and inventive advice, and a few breaks, some lofty goals can be reached. The only reason I'm writing this book is to help all of you young pitchers out there. You can be better than you are at present. You can improve in all the departments of pitching if you will listen to what I have to say.

I've been around, and looking at, pitchers most of my life. In this book, I am not excerpting any portion of the grand picture of successful pitching. It's all here, the old worthwhile practices, and my new inventive ideas. I can only ask that you try them.

For a few minutes, I want to return to Little League baseball. Today, I watched another few innings of the national tournament and I just could not believe what I was seeing. A very young left-hander throwing as many curveballs as fastballs. Imagine, a youngster of that age testing his arm in that manner. Earlier I talked about the win factor in youth league baseball. Far too many coaches are telling young pitchers, "We cannot beat this team unless you throw something other than fastballs. Go out there and use your curveball."

The announcers, certainly they should know better, but I hear them saying, "What a fine curveball this boy has had today. It really sets up his fastball." Through the years there have been ex pro players in the broadcasting booth and apparently they find no fault in these very young pitchers bending off curveballs.

The human arm was not placed there to throw a baseball. Fastballs at any age can be a test for any arm, but to throw a number of curveballs when a pitcher is 11 or 12 years of age is pure suicide. I have always recommended that no pitcher throw curveballs until at least 15 or 16 years of age. A curveball can be taught to a pitcher in a matter of days, so why the big hurry. The answer, of course, is to win at any age, regardless of the physical consequences. I know there are coaches in youth baseball who feel as I do, thank heaven for that, but there are far too many who do not understand what can happen on a single pitch. When the elbow and the shoulder are pushed to the limit, using undeveloped tendons and muscles recklessly, only bad things can happen.

There should be a rule in Little League baseball prohibiting any pitcher from throwing a breaking pitch. Let the pitchers throw their fastballs and let the chips fall where they may. Let them work on the control, their motion, fielding, and the rest. I'm sure there would be more runs scored, but certainly more arms saved.

Since we're discussing arms, I'll close this chapter with some good advice about proper care of that left or right pitching limb. As I mentioned earlier, never throw with a sore arm, or a stiff arm. Never go out on the field, pick up a ball, and without warming up, throw it a great distance. If you are a pitcher playing another position for your club, make sure you warm up each inning before the action starts. I have seen pitchers playing in the outfield make a long throw without taking a single warm up throw between innings. All outfielders should take turns at taking a baseball out with them between innings and make a throw or two while the pitcher takes his warm-ups.

Young pitchers should never fool around with a screwball. That particular pitch is extremely hard on the arm and should never be attempted until he is well along in his career. The same should be the rule for any split finger type of pitch.

I have had letters from young pitchers asking about the knuckle ball. If you can throw that pitch with good movement, and you can throw it consistently for a strike (very few pitchers can), then by all means add it to your collection of pitches. It will not hurt your arm for it is thrown at a low rate of speed with very little effort. Speaking for myself, I could throw a nice knuckle ball on the

63

sidelines but never used it in a game because I could not keep it in the strike zone. In the big leagues, I can only recall four or five pitchers in the past twenty years with a well controlled knuckle ball.

Always have in mind, in regards to the number of different pitches you throw during a game, it is far better to have three pitches with great command, than to have five with just average control.

Now and then, I have had questions from young pitchers about throwing underhanded. There have been several in the big leagues through the years and I can remember three or four having outstanding success. It can be tough on hitters for the angle of delivery is so much different than all the others. If you can throw from down under with some velocity (you should try to sink your fastball), and can throw strikes, then give it a try. The hardest delivery (angle) for a pitcher is the over the top motion. The easiest, the underhanded delivery (here I'm talking about the stress on the arm). The one drawback to the underhanded angle is the flatness of the slider or curveball. With no down spin, it's ineffective most of the time.

Take a rest and return with enthusiasm for chapter 12.

Chapter 12

For a number of years, I have gotten into my car and visited public sites of education expressing my views about the importance of reading and writing, and the beauty and grace of our American writers and poets from the 19th century. In such a short period of time (from 1860 – 1900), we lost Longfellow, Emerson, Lowell, Holmes, Irving, Poe, Cooper, and Whittier, just to name a few. In my judgment, these classic literary giants have never been replaced. There is a mellifluous song in Longfellow's poetry; a magnificent excitement in Cooper's stories of Indians along the Mohawk; and there is peace and longing in the homespun lines of Whittier's "**SNOWBOUND**".

For me, there has always been a kinship between these great writers and our classic baseball starters from the past. Has there ever been a modern pitcher to replace the artistic and durable talents of one Walter Johnson, the big train of the Washington Senators? How about the fantastic exploits of that wonderful left-hander, Warren Spahn? Johnson won over 400 games, and Spahn more than any other southpaw, 368. Between them, they recorded nearly 11,000 innings, and over 900 complete games. They had the courage and heart of an American frontiersman, and the toughness and durability of Red Grange, and Dick Butkus. They were followed by the likes of Bob Feller, Early Wynn, Nolan Ryan, Bob Lemon, Tom Seaver, Don Sutton, and some others of equal talent. But now the days of that type of pitcher have all but vanished, faded as a morning mist before the warm rays of the sun. There recently has been Roger Clemens, a 300 game winner, and perhaps one or two others in the next year or so, and then it's all over. The five man rotation has put the damper on future 300 game winners. So many of the modern pitchers will find their games thrown away by relief men. Check the box scores in your daily newspaper to get the true picture. Gone also is the great pride of accomplishment within our present day hurlers. Today, I see pitcher after pitcher generously giving up the baseball to a manager after five innings of work. He walks quickly to the dugout where he's greeted by the bench players and the pitching coach, all of whom congratulate him on an evening's long labor of five or six innings. What personal pride must be running through the veins of that young man!

As I have mentioned earlier, but it is well worth mentioning once again, it is essential to the complete makeup of man and woman that our life's work contains a challenge, a fair amount of self-pride that will carry us over the rough times. We have some fine relief pitchers, but a couple of innings in middle relief, or a closer getting a save when he allows a run or two in a single inning, is no substitute for the hardworking complete game starter. Many of our fine young arms are being wasted by throwing fifty or sixty innings per season. In my time, this great bundle of talent would have been placed on the mound as starters with the opportunity to pitch themselves into the Baseball Hall of Fame.

The modern day pitcher is not entirely to blame for this dilemma. In the minor leagues, young pitchers should be working more innings as starters. They should be working more innings in spring training. You cannot expect young pitchers to go nine innings in the big leagues when they have not been prepared in the minors. It tears me up to see these clubs bring up a promising young man with a 94 mile per hour fastball, a late breaking curveball, and stick all of that promise into the bullpen. What a waste of natural talent.

There is another important point that I would like to return to for a few paragraphs. Arm care, and how it relates to modern day baseball. Unfortunately, there are managers today who live by the arms in their bullpen. I have made a close observation in recent years and the results are truly disturbing. Many managers have no qualms about using a young arm three or four days in a row. The particular manager I have in mind managed in the big leagues for a great number of years, for two different clubs, and the number of promising arms he ruined out of the bullpen is most frightening. Night after night, he would call on the same pitcher until at last the pitcher could no longer pitch hurt and would ask to be set down. You see, managers understand that it runs against the grain of any competitor to complain, to make excuses, even when your arm seems to be hanging near your knees. What will my teammates think of my refusal to come in for an inning or so in a tight ballgame? Many managers take that advantage and run with it. In my day, the managers had no such problems with their bullpen for it was seldom used. As I have mentioned earlier, there is no greater risk to one's arm than warming up night after night in the bullpen, at times coming into the games, and on other occasions just wearing down the arm. The arm needs complete rest over a certain time period and only the starters have that opportunity.

Perhaps now and then there is a young man in the system with what is called a rubber arm. I have seen a few in my day, and I have no qualms about that young man using his unusual gift to make his way into the big leagues. But to say almost all young pitchers fall into that category is absolutely absurd.

So, again my young friends, you must protect yourself in this era of reliefitus. You have but a single arm to throw a baseball, and a single pitch at the wrong time may very well end your career. You must never be bashful about speaking up when your arm is tired or hurting. The uncaring manager or pitching coach will, of course, live for another season, and you must make sure you live also. Strive to be a starting pitcher to protect your arm; never throw when your arm is stiff or you have soreness; and as I have mentioned several times, do not throw breaking balls until you have reached the age of 16.

I have touched lightly on the subject of passiveness and how it could very well prevent you from becoming a great pitcher. Never accept any effort on the mound unless you have given it your very best quality and quantity of mental and physical endeavor. Do not accept advice from others, no matter their position, unless you carefully analyze that advice and it makes sense to you and your career. I have watched as pitching coaches changed young pitchers' deliveries into something totally unfit for their natural makeup, thereby causing a sore arm and a risk of permanent injury. Use your intelligence, and remember that no one knows your body like yourself. Be forceful with your personality, make your own decisions, use sound judgment, and your pitching will speak for itself.

In 1950, I was placed on a ball club in the Kansas-Oklahoma-Missouri League. I was but nineteen years of age and I was far from being called passive. I knew my potential and I knew the path I needed to follow to reach the big leagues. I reported to the ball club from an eastern league and met the manager, who shall remain anonymous, and I was ready to resume my career.

Even before I signed my first contract with the Yankees, it was understood by both parties that I would never be able to pitch every day, or every other day, in relief. I'm sure this particular manager was informed of the understanding but instead he marked me for the bullpen. I explained my position in pleasant terms but he refused to listen and placed me on the bench for a lengthy amount of time. I was not about to give in for to me an agreement was something to be honored. To make a long story a short one, the manager was fired and I started the second evening after the new skipper took over. I'm sure there were a number of reasons why this manager was fired, but keeping me on the bench did not help his case.

Now for another important pointer about pitching. Many times I have been asked by young pitchers about the merits of throwing a baseball from two different angles. Perhaps you throw three quarter and wonder about dropping down and coming sidearm now and then, or you throw directly overhand and want to show the hitter something sidearm. There are several things to consider before you take that action in an actual game. To start with, you must have at least two pitches from each delivery so the hitter cannot look for a certain pitch. Next, you must have good control of those two or more pitches. Lastly, you must remember that sidearm pitches from a right-handed pitcher to a left-handed hitter are seldom successful, at least they are not recommended.

My delivery was from a high three quarter angle and 99% of my pitches came from that position. However, once in a while I would drop down to a sidearm angle while facing a tough right-handed hitter. When I came sidearm, I sank my fastball, and used a sweeping curveball that I started at the hitter and broke it down across the outside corner, knee high. It is always an advantage for the pitcher to give the hitter another pitch or two to think about. I practiced the sidearm pitches on the sidelines between starts, and always threw a few in my warm-up pitches before I actually started a game. I never threw such pitches to a left-handed hitter.

If you are a left-handed pitcher and can come sidearm to the left-handed hitters, so much the better. Make sure your curveball stays away and not inside. Again, you must be able to control these pitches.

Before closing this chapter, I want to mention a game that I watched for a few minutes this afternoon. It delighted me to watch Nomo, the Japanese pitcher for the Dodgers. Check out his big windmill type of windup, all arms and legs, and he completely baffles the hitter with deception. As I have mentioned several times in earlier chapters, what a great advantage it is to have a non compact wind-up, using your entire body for leverage and deception. Nomo is a throw-back to the great pitchers of my era. He has a good shot at winning twenty games this season.

In the game mentioned above, I also took note of another pitcher, a right-hander for the opposition. Here was a gifted pitcher with a 95 mile per hour fastball and one of the best breaking balls in the National League. Out of the bullpen he came and worked one inning, his 60th appearance of the season. The inning meant little to the outcome of the game for his club was already a number of runs behind on the scoreboard. What a waste of talent, I thought, for years ago he would have been an outstanding starter. At six feet five and over two hundred pounds, he has the perfect physical build for the long haul. In his present role, he will be fortunate to win more than a couple of games all season.

Again, it's break time. So, stretch those legs, wiggle your toes, and straighten that spine. Chapter 13 awaits you.

Chapter 13

As a closing chapter, I would like to mention the pitchers' role in the American and National League 2003 playoffs.

There is no criticism on my part of the pitchers involved in these games. All have worked hard in earlier years to reach this high plateau of professional baseball. But I do want to point out why a number of these pitchers lost games, both in the ALCS and the NLCS.

Through this entire book, I have talked of the need for a better strike zone for pitchers. If you were watching these games, I'm sure you remarked a number of times, "Why that pitch was right at the hitter's waist level and it was called a ball." Of course it was, and you were correct in showing your disgust. Most base on balls in our present setup are caused by the miniature strike zone. Anytime the pitcher gets behind in the count, he's asking for trouble, for most pitchers it means giving the hitter a fastball to hit. Always remember, the pitch count regarding balls and strikes usually determines the final outcome of the game. I could see no difference in the strike zone of the various plate umpires. Although there has been much talk this season about giving the pitchers a higher strike zone, little has changed. Hitters continue to take, and take, and take, until they have the advantage in the ball and strike count. In many instances, a walk is fully as important as a base hit. In the Chicago Cubs/Florida Marlins contest (sixth game of the playoffs), Prior walked the first two batters in the 8th inning and both scored in the 8 run fiasco.

Prior is a great talent, one of the best I've seen in a number of years. In my judgment, he simply ran out of gas in that 8th inning. Once again, in my judgment, it was not his fault. Let's look at the facts leading up to that late season outing. During the regular season, he was seldom ever allowed to pitch nine innings. How can you ask a starting pitcher to go the entire route when he's almost entirely unfamiliar with going the distance? Of course, in the playoffs and in the World Series, managers want to keep their best pitchers in the game as long as possible. The reason being that most relief pitchers have been over-worked during the regular season, and now when needed the most, prove to be ineffective.

The solution, as I've mentioned in earlier chapters, is to groom the starting pitchers to go the entire route in the minor leagues. Once up to the parent club, let them pitch a complete game as soon as possible. With a five man rotation, these pitchers will be strong at the close of the season.

Prior was not the only great pitcher to run out of gas in the late innings. Martinez, of the Red Sox, pitched well into the 8th inning against the Yankees, and then was hit hard. I watched both pitchers very closely and it was obvious that they were tired. Pitches started to be high in the strike zone, and far too many caught too much of the plate.

In previous chapters, I have dwelled upon the importance of running, of building up leg strength, so pitchers can be sharp with their control in the late innings. I've also mentioned the importance of going nine innings to build up arm strength, and developing confidence. To my recollection, of the 28 starting pitchers in the ALCS and the NLCS, only one finished the job. Only a single pitcher had the great satisfaction of saying, "I started and I finished. What a great feeling."

Within this book, I have preached the importance of retiring the first hitter in the inning and the importance of not allowing runs to be scored in the first innings. Yet, even the best pitchers in the big leagues, time after time, failed in their assignments. Their ball club was put in a position of playing "catch-up" for the next eight innings.

I wrote earlier about making every pitch count. Yet, in many of these games, pitchers nibbled around the plate, wasting pitches, and often ended up walking the hitters. The only time I ever nibbled around the plate was when I had a two strike and no ball count on the hitter. I feel that's sound advice for any pitcher, at any level of competition.

Some chapters ago, I talked of the importance of having a nice big windup to help velocity, and to bring deception into the pitcher's arsenal. The only pitcher to use such a valuable asset was Dontrelle

Willis of the Marlins. Using a big windup of arms and legs, he pitched well in the first game of the World Series. When I pitched, most pitchers used such a windup and, in my opinion, that concept of delivering the baseball should never have been discarded.

I noticed several pitchers in the playoffs delivering the baseball without the help of their entire body. Pitchers throwing as infielders. Brad Penny threw from the first base side of the rubber, something that makes no sense whatsoever to me. He has a better than average curveball, but its effectiveness is limited to right-handed hitters when he fails to take advantage of the angle of the right side of the rubber. In my day, I never knew a single right handed pitcher that threw from the first base side of the rubber.

In the playoffs, we had several pitchers who helped themselves with the bat. Kerry Wood hit a two run homer, and Josh Beckett looked very good with a bat in his hands. I'm sorry to say that several pitchers need a great deal of work on their bunting.

All in all, the playoffs proved that hitting holds the upper hand over pitching. Most pitchers struggled, while the good share of hitters found little difficulty. Base hits were numerous, and homeruns continued to dog the hurlers. As always, there is a great imbalance between hitting and pitching.

Hopefully there will be changes made in future years regarding the strike zone. Perhaps the mound will be elevated to its proper position. Maybe the baseball will be dejuiced so only the legitimate homerun hitters will hit for the distance. Maybe the rules will be changed to allow pitchers to pitch inside without danger of banishment from the game.

However, no rule change will benefit the pitcher if he fails to perform in a winning manner. I just watched the first inning of the second game of the World Series. Mark Redmond, of the Marlins, had two outs, nobody on base, when he hit the next hitter with a pitch. After this mistake, he gave up a single, and then with the count three balls and no strikes, he gave the next hitter a fat fastball right in the middle of the plate that was crushed for a homerun. Three mistakes; three runs; enough said.

Fame, always a whimsical jade, can never be reached in baseball with those kinds of performances. Mark Redman, usually a fine performer, has a below average fastball for the big leagues, so he must pitch ballgames not only with his arm but also with his head. No pitcher should ever let up on a three and nothing fastball. I seldom ever found myself in that situation, but believe me, if I did I would have some mustard on the pitch. Hitters just wait for a cripple pitch aimed for the middle of the strike zone. Making mental mistakes on the mound will take some of the romance out of a very colorful profession. In professional baseball, it will also take a large fold of money out of your wallet.

In the writing profession, it is a habit to sit down to work for a couple of hours after dinner and find oneself searching for the right words well past two o'clock in the morning. This, of course, exemplifies the fascination of the work. This writer has sat at the typewriter the entire night and the next day felt but little more fatigued than if he had been in bed.

Baseball, for me, holds the same fascination. Babe Ruth seems alive and well. Tales of his exploits have persisted for eighty some odd years and have been so vividly colored by his chroniclers that the Babe seems almost too good to be true.

Baseball is like one's sweetheart, all much alike, yet each with distinguishing features that only the lover remembers. The game has magnificent traits of science, and overpowering moments of charm and ruggedness. It is a gateway to dreams, and one of this country's most precious commodities. Writing of baseball brings forth rich, melancholy sentences. For most writers, the words peal outward like the sound of country bells, falling sweetly and sadly on the ear.

So my young friends, I close these chapters with much regret, for the journey has been a trip of great enjoyment. As a pitcher, always remember each game presents an opportunity for improvement. Also to be remembered is the inner strength the game provides. It is beauty without vanity, strength without arrogance, courage without maliciousness.

If you give the game all you have to offer, the game will reward you with a touch of glory, and a warm inner satisfaction, unknown in so many other professions.

Epilogue

I have mentioned a time or two, that I do not enjoy pulling my own strings, lauding my own achievements, or asking puffs from others. However, I feel it's important for you to have a descriptive report of what I wanted for my final destination, and the great solace I gained from trying to get there. Everyone should have dreams, always traveling in an orbit that intersects the plane of the modern earth. We should have fertility of mind, an abundance of resources, and a variety of knowledge, which leaves footprints at every door. We should strive to have a set of bookshelves in our brain where every volume is in its proper place.

As each day passes, it is very clear to me that the art of pitching becomes more difficult. The imbalance between hitting and pitching is constantly widening. Hits allowed; earn run average; homeruns given up; base on balls; all of these monsters for the pitcher continue to climb. Changes in equipment have greatly benefited the men in the batter's box.

Pitchers must come up with some new ideas, and regenerate some of the valued old theories, if they hope to finish a season with a winning record. Last evening, I watched two of the top clubs in the major leagues and a total of eleven pitchers were used in a 12-8 game. Not a single pitcher on either side was impressive. All of those pitchers committed mistakes that I have discussed in this book. Poor pitch selection, far too many pitches at the waist level, wildness, fielding lapses, and the list goes on and on. In my judgment, not a single hurler entered the game with a plan for disposing of hitters.

I never walked to the mound without a game plan. As pitchers, you must be enriched by broader experience, sounder in judgment, and mellower in temperament, to outperform hitters. There is great

74

wisdom in the words from the past, the tales told by former great pitchers such as Bob Feller. I have listened to Dizzy Dean, Hal Newhouser, and Feller, all in the Hall of Fame, and found myself nearly speechless before the stupendous wisdom of their words. The past is never something to be forgotten, rather, it is an enormous pit of information to be tapped and rejuvenated for present conditions.

Baseball is a great tool for fresh comfort and new enterprises for self-development. It is a game woven together in a perfect sphere, a game so precise that the smallest change alters its very being.

When I was but a child of ten years, I would sit in one of the dugouts at the little baseball field near my parent's home and listen to the far away whistles of the Michigan Central trains. I wondered if perhaps some day I would be aboard one of those trains heading out into a world of great adventure and excitement. In a small village of a few hundred people it seemed unlikely, but baseball took me all over this country, and into several others, as an active professional player, and a scouting supervisor searching for talent. I owe much of my success in life to baseball and the many doors it opened for me over some sixty years.

If you have a strong right or left arm, enriched with natural born baseball talent, you too can make such a journey, and the length and width of such an expedition depends on the effort, the dedication, and the sacrifices you are willing to make. If the arm is there, the great love for the game present, the sky is the limit.

Babe Ruth has always been one of my heroes, not only for his tremendous skills as a baseball player, but also for his endless attention to young people. He always had time for a youngster at the ballpark, out in the street, or at a hospital. No one could ever replace the Babe in such acts of kindness, but in my small way I have always tried to spend time with kids all over the country. There is an old and beautiful quote that says, "No man stands taller than when he stoops to help a child." It is quite easy talking with these great kids about our wonderful game, for if you love it as I do, I say the right thing, find the right word, and get the correct meaning.

So, for all of you kids, young and old, I hope I have convinced you that baseball is something very special. It builds character, breeds great work habits, and can bring you a pleasure unfelt in most other game endeavors. There is a great deal to be said about always giving everything you do in this life one hundred percent. I shall be watching your progress in baseball with devouring and triumphant eagerness.

About the Author

In high school Ken Beardslee set seven national pitching records. He still holds the best percentage of strikeouts for a single high school season, and for an entire high school career (for one season, 19 strikeouts for every 21 batters faced. For a career, 18 strikeouts for every 21 batters faced). No other high school pitcher in the nation has been able to match those feats. All of Ken's high school pitching records may be found in the yearly edition of the National High School Sports Record Book, published by the National Federation of State High School Associations in Kansas City, Missouri.

As a pitcher in the New York Yankee organization, Ken won a total of 64 games while losing but 24. Rising from Class D to AAA classification in a little over three years, he set strikeout records in two different minor leagues.

When his active playing career was ended by an injury, he joined the Pittsburgh Pirate scouting department where he remained for over twenty years. He became a scouting supervisor handling all scouting operations in the Midwest.

Besides his writing, Ken pursues an active role in public speaking, appearing before large audiences in Michigan and Indiana.

Printed in the United States
67757LVS00005B/475-573

9 781418 431808